The Polymyalgia Rheumatica Diet

Susan Parker, MAT

Copyright 2014 by Susan Parker. All Rights Reserved.

ISBN: 978-1497384859

Contents

Introduction 3

Dinners 7

Side Dishes 43

Breakfasts 75

Lunch 85

Desserts 127

Snacks 131

Index 135

Introduction

Polymyalgia rheumatica might mean that you are suffering from chronic pain right now – but with the right medications and proper diet, it doesn't have to stay that way. Currently, the main treatment for polymyalgia rheumatica is corticosteroid medication, usually prednisone. This medication comes with a long list of unwanted side-effects, from the mild (stomach upset, increased, hunger, insomnia) to the severe (high blood pressure, diabetes and brittle bones).

Many studies have shown that dietary changes, along with exercise and stress-reduction can actually be an effective way to treat the condition. This can lead to a reduction or even elimination of medications.

This isn't a Fad Diet!

Beware of fad diets that promise to alleviate your polymyalgia rheumatic symptoms. According to the National Institute of Arthritis and Musculoskeletal and Skin Diseases, these diets have never been shown to be effective in any clinical study. However, the Institute does recommend that you follow a "proper diet." What's a "proper" diet? A diet rich in whole grains, vegetables, fruits and lean meat with sufficient calcium intake. Certain foods should be restricted or eliminated entirely: sugar, salt, caffeine and alcohol. As far as protein is concerned, the bulk of your protein intake should be from fish and calcium-rich foods like low-fat cheese and low-fat yogurt. The elimination of red meat (including pork) can be a challenge for some – especially if you're used to the typical American fast food diet. This cookbook concentrates on fish as a protein source. You also won't find any gluten – another ingredient you should avoid if you have PMR. Gluten can be found in flour, wheat products (including gluten-free bread, pizza and spaghetti). Gluten has been linked to many arthritic-related disorders and eliminating it from your diet *may* make your symptoms completely disappear. Hafstrom et. Al, in their research study on gluten-free diets, had this to say about dietary changes and rheumatoid arthritis (RA and PMR are very similar diseases): "dietary modification may be of clinical benefit for certain RA patients, and that this benefit may be related to a reduction in immunoreactivity to food antigens eliminated by the change in diet."

Following a low-fat, low-meat diet reduces your risk of developing giant cell arteritis – a serious complication of PMR.

A Note on Oils

For decades, we've been warned about the dangers of excess fats and oils in our diets. As a PMR patient, you should avoid fats and oils whenever possible – you can obtain "good" fats by eating avocados and replacing the oils in your kitchen with heart-healthy alternatives, like olive oil. All of the recipes found in this book use olive oil, and vegan margarine (now widely available in grocery stores – check ingredients for lurking hydrogenated oils).

How to use this book

In addition to the recipes in this book, you can eat unlimited:

- Fruits and Vegetables (preferably uncooked and unprocessed)
- Nuts – all kinds, including peanut vegan butter (without salt and sugar)
- Low fat dairy (milk, yogurt, cheese etc.)
- Fortified orange juice

- Other fruit juices and fruit juice smoothies (check for no added sugar)
- Gluten-free crackers and gluten-free breads
- Raw food products. Check out your local natural foods store. Most stores will carry a variety of raw food products including chips, crackers, cookies, cakes and meals.
- Gluten-free cereals with low-fat milk (preferably non-dairy milk like soy milk or rice milk).
- Legumes
- Rice
- Lentils
- Eggs (egg whites are preferable as they are lower in fat, but the occasional egg dish is ok).
- Tofu
- Gluten-free vegetarian meat substitutes (like Marjon "hamburger" crumbles).
- Seafood – all types, without regular (wheat) breading.
- Lean baked chicken without the skin.
- Gluten-free pasta (rice, corn or quinoa) and pasta sauces (low fat, low salt, no added sugar).
- Changing your diet is a process – it's difficult to radically change your diet overnight. However, following the recipes included in this book will help you tailor your diet towards that "proper" diet that's recommended by medical professionals.

Reference: Hafström et. Al. *A vegan diet free of gluten improves the signs and symptoms of rheumatoid arthritis: the effects on arthritis correlate with a reduction in antibodies to food antigens.*

http://www.ncbi.nlm.nih.gov/pubmed/11600749

Dinners

Lemon Vegan butter Red Snapper
8 servings

If you haven't tried red snapper before, it's a Caribbean staple with a firm, meaty texture. I actually prefer to cook a whole red snapper, but they are rarely available in the grocery store. You should be able to find red snapper fillets in the freezer section.

Ingredients
3 lbs red snapper fillets
rice flour
pinch garlic powder and pepper
1/4 cup olive oil
4 tablespoons vegan butter
2 tablespoons lemon juice
2 tablespoons fresh snipped parsley

Procedure
1. Pat the fillets dry. Roll the fish lightly in flour mixed with garlic powder and pepper.
2. Heat oil in skillet; cook fish until brown on both sides (3 minutes per side).
3. Remove fish to platter and keep warm.
4. Add vegan butter and lemon to skillet; simmer one minute.
5. Pour mixture over the fish.
6. Sprinkle with fresh snipped parsley.

Prep: 5 mins
Cook: 8 mins
Ready: 13 mins
Nutrition:
Calories 359.5
Carbohydrates 0.3 g
Fat 15.0 g
Protein 40.5 g

Roasted Caribbean Red Snapper

4 servings

If you like lots of flavor on your fish, this is the dish for you. It works really well with a side of home-made tartar sauce: mix ¼ cup vegan mayo, 3T spicy brown mustard, 2T pickle relish and 1T crushed capers in a bowl.

Ingredients
2 tablespoons grated fresh ginger
1 garlic clove, minced
1 serrano chile, seeded and minced
1 teaspoon fresh chopped thyme
1/8 teaspoon ground allspice
1 tablespoon olive oil, plus more for rubbing
Pinch pepper

Procedure
1. Preheat oven to 425°.
2. Combine all of the ingredients except for the sea garlic powder.
3. Make 5 parallel slashes on each side of the red snapper. Slice almost all the way through to the bone.
4. Rub the paste into the fish, making sure to get most of the paste in the slashes.
5. Baste the fish all over with olive oil and sprinkle with the pepper.
6. Transfer the fish to a deep baking pan. Roast the fish for about 30 minutes (you may need a little more, or less time depending on the size of the snapper), until the flesh just flakes. Transfer the fish to a platter and serve.

Active: 10 MIN **Total Time:** 40 MIN

Nutrition (Note: this is approximate as it will depend on the size of the snapper):

Nutrition:
Calories 359.5
Carbohydrates 0.3 g
Fat 15.0 g
Protein 40.5 g

Lemon Baked Cod
4 servings

Make sure you use fresh-squeezed lemon with this recipe. The lemon is the mainstay flavor here, so if you use the little lemon-squeeze bottles you won't get a good flavor at all.

Ingredients

1 lb cod fillets
1/4 cup vegan butter, melted
2 tablespoons fresh-squeezed lemon juice
1/4 cup rice flour
1/2 teaspoon garlic powder
1/8 teaspoon white pepper
paprika
Parsley sprigs and lemon wedges for garnish

Procedure

1. Cut fillets into serving size pieces.
2. Mix the vegan butter and lemon juice.
3. Mix flour, garlic powder and white pepper in a separate bowl.
4. Dip fish into vegan butter mixture and then coat with the flour mixture.
5. Place fish in an ungreased 8" square baking pan.
6. Pour remaining vegan butter mixture over fish and then sprinkle with paprika.
7. Cook uncovered in 350 degree oven until fish flakes easily with fork, 25-30 minutes. Garnish with parsley sprigs and lemon slices if desired.

Prep: 10 mins
Cook: 25 mins
Ready: 35 mins
Nutrition:
Calories 225.2
Carbohydrates 6.5 g
Fat 12.3 g
Protein 21.2 g

Dijon Baked Cod
4 servings

This has a lot more tang than the milder (but still good!) lemon baked cod. Dijon mustard has a tremendous amount of flavor in small amounts. My favorite is Grey Poupon.

Ingredients
1/4 cup low-fat mayonnaise
2 teaspoons Dijon mustard
2 teaspoons horseradish (jarred)
1 tablespoon fresh-squeezed lemon juice
1/8 cup gluten-free breadcrumbs
1 tablespoon parmesan cheese
4 (6 ounce) cod fillets
1 tablespoon vegan butter
1/4 cup gluten-free breadcrumbs
1 tablespoon parmesan cheese

Procedure
1. Preheat oven to 350°F and lightly grease a baking sheet.
2. Mix low-fat mayonnaise, mustard, horseradish and lemon juice in a small bowl; stir in parmesan cheese and 1/8 cup of gluten-free bread crumbs.
3. Arrange fish portions on prepared cooking sheet, spread mixture evenly over fish.
4. Mix melted vegan butter, gluten-free bread crumbs and 1 tablespoon parmesan cheese in a bowl. Sprinkle over the cod.
5. Bake for 15-20 minutes until cod flakes easily with a fork.
6. **Prep:** 5 mins

Cook: 15 mins
Ready: 20 mins
Nutrition:
Calories 283.5
Carbohydrates 11.5 g
Fat 10.3 g
Protein 34.4 g

Chili, Cumin and Lime Cod
2 - 4 servings

The great thing about cod is that its mild flavor makes it extremely versatile. You'll never get bored of the possibilities. I actually double up on the spices in this recipe, although more spice isn't for everyone! I used Mexican chili powder (available in the Hispanic section of the grocery store).

Ingredients
2 lbs fresh cod fillets
1 teaspoon chili powder
1/2 teaspoon fresh chopped cilantro
1/2 teaspoon garlic powder
2 tablespoons vegan butter
1/4 teaspoon cumin
1 lime, juiced

Procedure
1. Preheat oven to 450°F.
2. Coat a baking dish with cooking spray. Place cod in pan.
3. Sprinkle chili powder and garlic powder over fish.
4. Roast 5-7 minutes until opaque and fish flakes easily with a fork.
5. Melt vegan butter in small saucepan.
6. Add cilantro, cumin and lime juice and cook for 1 more minute.
7. Before serving drizzle vegan butter mixture over cod.

Prep: 10 mins
Cook: 7 mins
Ready: 17 mins
Nutrition:
Calories 485.6
Carbohydrates 2.8 g
Fat 14.8 g
Protein 81.4 g

Crabmeat Stuffed Haddock
6 servings

The extra effort to prepare the stuffing for the haddock is well worth it. Not only does it taste amazing, it looks great too. Good enough for a special occasion!

Ingredients
- 3 tablespoons olive oil
- 1 stalk celery, finely chopped
- 3 green onions, finely chopped
- 1 teaspoon minced garlic
- 1 (6 ounce) can lump crabmeat, drained
- 3 slices dry white gluten-free bread, crusts removed and cubed
- 1/4 teaspoon garlic powder
- 1/4 teaspoon ground black pepper
- 1 egg, beaten
- 1/2 cup grated low-fat Romano cheese
- 2 tablespoons lemon juice
- 1 tomato, seeded and diced
- 1/8 teaspoon ground black pepper
- 5 tablespoons vegan butter, melted
- 6 (4 ounce) haddock fillets
- Toothpicks

Procedure
1. Preheat oven to 375 degrees F. Lightly grease a 9x13 inch baking dish.
2. Heat olive oil in a heavy skillet over medium heat for 2-3 minutes. Add celery, green onion and garlic.
3. Stir fry for 3-4 minutes until soft. Remove from heat, and stir in the crabmeat, gluten-free bread cubes, egg, Romano cheese, lemon juice, and tomato. Season with garlic powder and 1/4 teaspoon of pepper. Mix until well blended.
4. Lay the haddock fillets in the prepared baking dish. Brush with melted vegan butter. Place a generous tablespoon of the crab mixture onto half of each fillet, and fold the other half over to cover. Secure with toothpicks. Sprinkle on any remaining stuffing, and drizzle with any leftover melted vegan butter. Cover the dish with aluminum foil.
5. Bake for 20 minutes. Remove the cover and bake for an additional 10 minutes, until the top has browned and the fish flakes easily with a fork.

Prep: 15mins
Cook: 40 mins
Ready: 55 mins
Nutrition:
Calories 365 kcal
Carbohydrates 9 g
Fat 21.5 g
Protein 32.9 g

Seafood a la Creole

6 servings

I have been on vacation to New Orleans a dozen times. And my favorite part of the vacation is the food! This seafood Creole dish is probably my favorite New Orleans style dish. It's fairly mild, but very flavorful.

Ingredients

3/4 teaspoon dried oregano
1/2 teaspoon garlic powder
1/2 teaspoon ground white pepper
1/2 teaspoon ground black pepper
1/2 teaspoon cayenne pepper
1/2 teaspoon fresh thyme, chopped
1/2 teaspoon fresh sweet basil
1/4 cup vegan butter
1 cup peeled and chopped tomato
3/4 cup chopped onion
3/4 cup chopped celery
3/4 cup chopped green bell pepper
1 1/2 teaspoons minced garlic
1 1/4 cups fish stock
1 cup canned tomato sauce
1 teaspoon agave nectar
1/2 teaspoon hot pepper sauce (I like Chalula)
2 bay leaves
1 pound peeled and deveined shrimp
1 pound bay scallops
1 pound haddock fillets cut into bite-sized pieces

Procedure

1. Mix the oregano, garlic powder, white pepper, black pepper, cayenne pepper, thyme, and basil in a small bowl.
2. Melt vegan butter in a large skillet over medium heat; stir in tomato, onion, celery, green bell pepper, and garlic. Stir-fry until the onion is translucent, about 5 minutes.
3. Stir in fish stock, tomato sauce, agave, hot pepper sauce, and bay leaves. Reduce heat to low and bring sauce to a simmer. Stir in seasoning mix and simmer until the flavors have blended, about 20 minutes.
4. Gently stir in shrimp, bay scallops, and haddock; bring sauce back to a simmer and cook until the shellfish and fish are opaque, about 20 more minutes. Remove bay leaves to serve.

Prep: 30 mins

Cook: 40 mins
Ready: in 1 hr 10 mins
Nutrition:
Calories   328 kcal
Carbohydrates   11.8 g
Fat 10 g
Protein 47.2 g

Baked Haddock
4 servings

This is a simple dish that only takes minutes to prepare. Dinner can be on the table in under half an hour!

Ingredients
3/4 cup milk
2 teaspoons garlic powder
3/4 cup gluten-free bread crumbs
1/4 cup grated Parmesan cheese
1/4 teaspoon fresh chopped thyme
4 haddock fillets
1/4 cup vegan butter, melted

Procedure
1. Preheat oven to 500 degrees F (260 degrees C).
2. In a small bowl, combine the milk and garlic powder. In a separate bowl, mix together the gluten-free bread crumbs, Parmesan cheese, and thyme. Dip the fillets in the milk, then press into the crumb mixture to coat.
3. Place fillets in a glass baking dish, and drizzle with melted vegan butter.
4. Bake on the top rack of the preheated oven until the fish flakes easily, about 15 minutes.

Prep: 10 mins
Cook: 15 mins
Ready: in 25 mins
Nutrition:
Calories   325 kcal
Carbohydrates   17 g
Fat   15.7 g
Protein   27.7 g

Parmesan-Lemon Tilapia
4 servings

Another fast dish you can whip up in minutes. The Spanish flavors will tingle your taste buds. Make sure you use fresh herbs whenever you can for maximum flavor.

Ingredients
4 (4 ounce) tilapia fillets
2 tablespoons sazon seasoning (sazon completa)
1 serving olive oil cooking spray
1/2 cup grated Parmesan cheese
2 tablespoons vegan butter, melted
1 1/2 tablespoons fat-free or low-fat mayonnaise
2 tablespoons fresh-squeezed lemon juice
2 teaspoons grated lemon zest
1/8 teaspoon fresh chopped basil
1/8 teaspoon ground black pepper
1/8 teaspoon onion powder
1/8 teaspoon garlic powder

Procedure
1. Preheat the broiler and set the oven rack about 6 inches from the heat Line a broiler pan with aluminum foil. Spray the broiler pan's rack with olive oil cooking spray.
2. Sprinkle tilapia with sazon seasoning and arrange on the prepared rack.
3. Cook the fillets under the broiler until fish is barely opaque, 2 to 3 minutes per side.
4. Mix the Parmesan cheese, vegan butter-margarine blend, fat-free low-fat mayonnaise, lemon juice, lemon zest, basil, black pepper, onion powder, and celery garlic powder together in a bowl.
5. Spread the Parmesan cheese blend over the fish fillets, return to oven, and continue cooking until the topping is golden brown and the fish flakes easily, 3 to 5 more minutes.

Prep: 15 mins
Cook: 10mins
Ready: 25 mins
Nutrition:
Calories 213 kcal
Carbohydrates 2.5 g
Fat 10.1 g
Protein 26.9 g

Baked Tilapia with Dill Sauce
4 servings
Ingredients
4 (4 ounce) tilapia filets
Garlic powder and pepper to taste
1 tablespoon Cajun seasoning (I like Emeril's)
1 lemon, thinly sliced
1/4 cup vegan low-fat mayonnaise
1/2 cup vegan sour cream
1/8 teaspoon garlic powder
1 teaspoon fresh lemon juice
2 tablespoons chopped fresh dill

Procedure
1. Mix together the low-fat mayonnaise, sour cream, garlic powder, lemon juice, dill and garlic powder in a small bowl. Place in the refrigerator.
2. Preheat the oven to 350 degrees F. Lightly grease a 9x13 inch baking dish.
3. Season the tilapia fillets with pepper and Cajun seasoning on both sides. Arrange the fillets in a single layer in the baking dish. Place a layer of lemon slices over the fillets.
4. Bake uncovered for 15 to 20 minutes in the preheated oven, or until fish flakes easily with a fork.
5. Serve the dill sauce with the tilapia.

Prep: 10 mins
Cook: 20 mins
Ready: in 30 mins

Nutrition:
Calories 284 kcal
Carbohydrates 5.7 g
Fat 18.6 g
Protein 24.5 g

Chipotle-Lime Fish Tacos 6 servings

Use the crunchy taco shells for this dish. The soft texture of the fish is a perfect opposite for the crunch of the shells. The extra large crunchy shells with a deep base (the ones that stand up) work best.

Ingredients
Marinade
1/4 cup extra virgin olive oil
2 tablespoons distilled white vinegar
2 tablespoons fresh-squeezed lime juice
2 teaspoons lime zest
1 1/2 teaspoons agave nectar
2 cloves garlic, minced
1/2 teaspoon cumin
1/2 teaspoon chili powder
1 teaspoon seafood seasoning, like Old Bay™
1/2 teaspoon ground black pepper
1 teaspoon hot pepper sauce (I like Chalula)
1 pound tilapia fillets, cut into chunks

Dressing
1 (8 ounce) container vegan sour cream
1/2 cup adobo sauce from chipotle peppers
2 tablespoons fresh squeezed lime juice
2 teaspoons lime zest
1/4 teaspoon cumin
1/4 teaspoon chili powder
1/2 teaspoon seafood seasoning
garlic powder and pepper to taste

Toppings
1 (10 ounce) package hard tacos
3 ripe tomatoes, seeded and diced
1 bunch cilantro, chopped
1 small head iceberg lettuce and shredded
2 limes, cut in wedges

Procedure
1. To make the marinade, whisk together the olive oil, vinegar, lime juice, lime zest, agave, garlic, cumin, chili powder, seafood seasoning, black pepper, and hot sauce in a bowl until blended. Place the tilapia in a shallow dish, and pour the marinade over the fish. Cover, and refrigerate 6 to 8 hours.

2. To make the dressing, combine the sour cream and adobo sauce in a bowl. Stir in the lime juice, lime zest, cumin, chili powder, seafood seasoning. Add garlic powder, and pepper in desired amounts. Cover, and refrigerate until needed.
3. Preheat a broiler. Set a broiler pan 4 inches from the heat.
4. Remove fish from marinade, drain off any excess and discard marinade. Broil fish pieces until easily flaked with a fork, turning once, about 2-3 minutes.
5. Assemble tacos by placing fish pieces in the center of tacos with desired amounts of tomatoes, cilantro, and lettuce; drizzle with dressing. Garnish with lime wedges.

Prep: 35 mins
Cook: 9 mins
Ready: 6 hrs 44 mins

Nutrition:
Calories 416 kcal
Carbohydrates 38.5 g
Fat 19.2 g
Protein 22.6 g

Fish Tacos with Honey-Cumin Cilantro Slaw and Chipotle Mayo
8 tacos

A second version of the fish tacos. They're so good I had to include two different recipes! This recipe uses the soft corn tortillas because the fried fish pieces give the dish the "crunch."

Ingredients
1 pound tilapia fillets, cut into chunks
1/2 cup fresh lime juice
1/3 cup fresh lime juice
2 tablespoons agave nectar
1 tablespoon olive oil
1 teaspoon ground cumin
1/2 cup vegan low-fat mayonnaise
2 chipotle chilies in adobo sauce
1 tablespoon adobo sauce from chipotle peppers
1/4 teaspoon garlic powder
1/8 teaspoon cayenne pepper
1/3 cup rice flour
2 eggs, beaten
2 cups gluten-free panko crumbs or gluten-free breadcrumbs
Garlic powder and ground black pepper to taste
1 cup olive oil for frying
2 cups shredded red cabbage
1 cup minced fresh cilantro leaves
8 (7 inch) corn tortillas, warmed

Procedure
1. Marinade the fish chunks in 1/2 cup lime juice. Cover, and refrigerate at least 4 hours.
2. Place the low-fat mayonnaise, chilies, adobo sauce, 1/4 teaspoon garlic powder, and cayenne pepper together in the bowl of a food processor. Pulse until smooth. Cover, and refrigerate.
3. Whisk together 1/3 cup lime juice, honey, olive oil, and ground cumin a small bowl. Set aside until needed.
4. Place the flour, eggs, and panko crumbs in three separate shallow dishes. Season the fish with garlic powder and pepper. Dip the fish pieces in the flour, coating evenly, and shaking off any excess. Dip in the eggs and then in the panko crumbs. Set the fish aside on a plate.
5. Pour 1 cup oil into a skillet to 1/4 inch deep. Heat the oil; place a tiny piece of gluten-free breading into the oil and heat the oil until the gluten-

free breading is sizzling. Cook the fish, turning two or three times until all sides are golden brown (about 4 or 5 minutes). The fish should flake easily with a fork. Drain on paper towels. Brush the fish with the lime-honey-cumin sauce.
6. Mix the cabbage and cilantro together in a bowl. Reserve 1/4 cup of the chipotle low-fat mayonnaise dressing, and pour the remaining dressing over the coleslaw mixture. Toss to coat evenly with the dressing.
7. Place the tortillas on a flat surface, and spread each with 1 tablespoon reserved chipotle low-fat mayonnaise dressing. Divide the fish between the tortillas. Top with the cilantro coleslaw.

Prep: 30 mins
Cook: 10 mins
Ready: 4 hrs 40 mins
Nutrition:
Calories   984 kcal
Carbohydrates   117.5 g
Fat   44.4 g
Protein 42.2 g

Goat Cheese stuffed Salmon
4 servings
Packed with protein, delicious and fast! What more could you want?
Ingredients
2t Dijon mustard
2T vegan low-fat mayonnaise
4 (4oz) salmon fillets
1/2 cup herbed low-fat goat cheese
garlic powder and pepper to taste

Procedure
1. Preheat oven to 350 degrees F (175 degrees C).
2. Mix the mustard and mayo together in a small bowl.
3. Lightly grease a large baking dish.
4. Arrange the salmon fillets in the baking dish. Make small incisions in each fillet, and stuff with equal amounts of the herbed goat cheese. Spread the mustard low-fat mayonnaise blend over each fillet. Season with garlic powder and pepper.
5. Bake salmon for 15 minutes in the preheated oven, or until easily flaked with a fork.

Prep: 15 mins
Cook: 15 mins
Ready: in 30 mins
Nutrition:
Calories 247 kcal
Carbohydrates 1.4 g
Fat 16.3 g
Protein 22.9 g

Pepper-Honey Cedar Plank Salmon

6 servings

A great tip I learned from kitchn.com: buy a cedar plank at Home Depot and have them cut the plank up into 8" pieces. It's a fraction of the cost of cedar planks you'll find in cooking stores. Make sure you soak the wood in water for a few hours before using. Although there's a lot of sweet (agave, pineapple juice and maple syrup), there's also a ton of protein.

Ingredients
- 2 (12 inch) untreated cedar planks
- 1/4 cup 100% pineapple juice
- 1/3 cup Bragg's liquid aminos
- 2 tablespoons white vinegar
- 2 tablespoons lemon juice
- 1 tablespoon olive oil
- 3/4 cup agave
- 1/4 cup maple syrup
- 1 teaspoon ground black pepper
- 1/2 teaspoon cayenne pepper
- 1/2 teaspoon paprika
- 1/4 teaspoon garlic powder
- 6 (6 ounce) skinless, boneless salmon fillets
- 1 pinch garlic powder and pepper to taste

Procedure
1. Bring the pineapple juice, Bragg's, vinegar, lemon juice, olive oil, and honey to a simmer in a medium saucepan over medium-high heat. Reduce the heat to medium-low, and stir in the maple syrup, 1 teaspoon black pepper, cayenne pepper, paprika, and garlic powder. Simmer, stirring occasionally, until the sauce has reduced to a syrupy consistency, about 15 minutes. Set the sauce aside.
2. Preheat an outdoor grill for medium heat. Place the planks on the grate. They are ready to cook on when they start to smoke and crackle.
3. Season the salmon with garlic powder and pepper. Place the fillets onto the smoking cedar planks, close the lid of the grill, and cook for 10 minutes. Spoon a small amount of the sauce over the salmon fillets, and continue cooking until the fish turns opaque in the center, about 5 minutes more. Drizzle the fish with sauce to serve.

Prep: 15 mins
Cook: 30 mins
Ready: in 1 hr 45 mins

Nutrition:
Calories   484 kcal
Carbohydrates   47.3 g
Fat 16.7 g
Protein   37 g

Marinated and Grilled Salmon

6 servings

The marinade for the fish gives it a sweet and tangy flavor, reminiscent of Chinese cooking.

Ingredients
1 1/2 pounds salmon fillets
lemon pepper to taste
garlic powder to taste
1/3 cup Bragg's liquid aminos
1/3 cup maple syrup
1/3 cup water
1/4 cup olive oil

Procedure
1. Season salmon fillets with lemon pepper, garlic powder, and garlic powder.
2. In a small bowl, stir together Bragg's liquid aminos, maple syrup, water, and olive oil. Place fish in a large ziplock bag with the Bragg's mixture, seal, and turn to coat. Refrigerate for at least 2 hours.
3. Preheat grill for medium heat.
4. Lightly oil grill grate. Place salmon on the preheated grill, and discard marinade. Cook salmon for 6 to 8 minutes per side, or until the fish flakes easily with a fork.

Prep: 15 mins
Cook: 16 mins
Ready: in 2 hrs 31 mins
Nutrition:
Calories 318 kcal
Carbohydrates 13.2 g
Fat 20.1 g
Protein 20.5 g

Mediterranean Salmon

4 servings

This dish goes perfect with a basic Caesar salad (lettuce, Parmesan, dressing and a sprinkle of croutons) or a Mediterranean salad (lettuce, olives, tomatoes, goat cheese, oil & balsamic dressing).

Ingredients
1/2 cup olive oil
1/4 cup balsamic vinegar
4 cloves garlic, pressed
4 (3 ounce) fillets salmon
1 tablespoon chopped fresh cilantro
1 tablespoon chopped fresh basil
1 1/2 teaspoons garlic powder

Procedure
1. Mix the olive oil and balsamic in a small bowl. Arrange the fillets in a shallow baking dish. Rub garlic onto the fillets and then pour the vinegar and oil over them, turning once to coat. Sprinkle with cilantro, basil, and garlic powder.
2. Preheat a broiler.
3. Place the salmon about 6 inches from the heat source, and broil for 15 minutes, turning once, or until browned on both sides. The fish should flake easily with a fork. Brush occasionally with the sauce from the pan.

Prep: 10 mins
Cook: 15 mins
Ready: 25 mins
Nutrition:
Calories 391 kcal
Carbohydrates 3.6 g
Fat 35.2 g
Protein 15 g

Peppered Shrimp Alfredo
4 servings
Quinoa pasta isn't as processed as the regular pasta you find in the grocery store, and it has a shake of protein too. It's gluten-free. Large grocery stores are starting to carry quinoa pasta, usually in the organic or green section of the store.

Ingredients
12 ounces quinoa pasta
1/4 cup vegan butter
2 tablespoons extra-virgin olive oil
1 onion, diced
2 cloves garlic, minced
1 red bell pepper, diced
1/2 pound portobello mushrooms, diced
1 pound shrimp, peeled and deveined
1 (15 ounce) jar low-fat Alfredo sauce
1/2 cup grated low-fat Romano cheese
1/2 cup coconut milk or cashew cream
1 teaspoon cayenne pepper, or more to taste
garlic powder and pepper to taste
1/4 cup chopped parsley

Procedure
1. Cook pasta according to package directions.
2. Meanwhile, melt vegan butter together with the olive oil in a saucepan over medium heat. Stir in onion, and cook until softened and translucent, about 2 minutes. Stir in garlic, red pepper, and mushroom; cook over medium-high heat until soft, about 2 minutes more.
3. Stir in the shrimp, and cook until firm and pink, then pour in Alfredo sauce, Romano cheese, and cream; bring to a simmer stirring constantly until thickened, about 5 minutes. Season with cayenne, garlic powder, and pepper to taste. Stir drained pasta into the sauce, and serve sprinkled with chopped parsley.

Prep: 30 mins
Cook: 20 mins
Ready: 50 mins
Nutrition:
Calories 707 kcal
Carbohydrates 50.6 g
Fat 45 g
Protein 28.4 g

Agave Grilled Shrimp
3 servings

Shrimp is another versatile staple. It's high in protein and low in calories. I'm lucky enough to live near a shrimp port (Mayport), so I have access to jumbo fresh shrimp. In a pinch, large shrimp from your grocery store will do, but if you can – try and find fresh jumbo shrimp. The texture is worth the effort.

Ingredients
1/2 teaspoon garlic powder
1/4 tablespoon ground black pepper
1/3 cup Worcestershire sauce
2 tablespoons dry white wine
2 tablespoons Italian-style salad dressing (sugar free)
1 pound large shrimp, peeled and deveined with tails attached
1/4 cup agave
1/4 cup vegan butter, melted
2 tablespoons Worcestershire sauce
skewers

Procedure
1. In a large bowl, mix together garlic powder, black pepper, 1/3 cup Worcestershire sauce, wine, and salad dressing; add shrimp, and toss to coat. Cover, and marinate in the refrigerator for 1 hour.
2. Preheat grill for high heat. Thread shrimp onto skewers, piercing once near the tail and once near the head. Discard marinade.
3. In a small bowl, stir together agave, melted vegan butter, and remaining 2 tablespoons Worcestershire sauce. Set aside for basting.
4. Lightly oil grill grate. Grill shrimp for 2 to 3 minutes per side, or until opaque. Baste occasionally with the honey-vegan butter sauce while grilling.

Prep: 30 mins
Cook: 6 mins
Ready: 1 hr 36 mins
Nutrition:
Calories 435 kcal
Carbohydrates 33.4 g
Fat 20.3 g
Protein 30 g

Grilled Marinated Shrimp

6 servings

Shrimp is a staple in my diet. A 3oz serving of shrimp is packed with 19 grams of protein.

Ingredients
1 cup olive oil
1/4 cup chopped fresh parsley
1 lemon, juiced
2 tablespoons hot pepper sauce (I like Chalula)
3 cloves garlic, minced
1 tablespoon tomato paste
2 teaspoons dried oregano
1 teaspoon garlic powder
1 teaspoon ground black pepper
2 pounds large shrimp, peeled and deveined with tails attached
skewers

Procedure
1. In a mixing bowl, mix together olive oil, parsley, lemon juice, hot sauce, garlic, tomato paste, oregano, garlic powder, and black pepper. Reserve a small amount for basting later. Pour remaining marinade into a large resealable plastic bag with shrimp. Seal, and marinate in the refrigerator for 2 hours.
2. Preheat the broiler for medium heat. Thread shrimp onto skewers, piercing once near the tail and once near the head. Discard marinade.
3. Lightly oil a broiling pan. Line the shrimp in the pan and then cook shrimp for 5 minutes per side, or until opaque, basting frequently with reserved marinade.

Prep: 30 mins
Cook: 10 mins
Ready: 2 hrs 40 mins

Nutrition:
Calories 447 kcal
Carbohydrates 3.7 g
Fat 37.5 g
Protein 25.3 g

Shrimp Curry
4 - 6 servings

You absolutely have to try making from-scratch curry! When I cut out sugar from my diet, it put a dent in the taste of food. I replaced it with spice – lots of spice of all kinds. That's why curry has become one of my favorite dishes. Curry doesn't have to be hot. The curry powder and jalapeno are what adds the spice, so adjust these ingredients if you want to tone down (or kick up) the spice.

Ingredients
5 cloves garlic
3-inch long piece fresh ginger, peeled
2 tablespoons olive oil
1/4 heaping teaspoon whole cloves
10 cardamom pods
8 whole allspice
1 cinnamon stick, broken in half
1 bay leaf
1 medium yellow onion, sliced
2 teaspoons curry powder
1/2 jalapeno, or more to taste
1/2 cup whole, peeled, canned tomatoes (with puree), roughly chopped
3/4 cup coconut milk
2 cups water
2 1/2 teaspoons garlic powder
1 1/2 pounds medium shrimp, peeled and deveined
2 tablespoons chopped fresh coriander leaves
1 tablespoon freshly squeezed lime juice

Procedure
1. Combine the garlic and ginger and puree into a paste in a food processor or with a mortar and pestle. Set aside.
2. Heat the oil in a large skillet over medium-high heat. Add the cloves, cardamom, allspice, cinnamon stick, and bay leaf. Stir fry until the cinnamon stick unfurls, about 30 seconds. Add the onion and stir fry until lightly browned, about 3 minutes.
3. Add the garlic-ginger paste, curry powder, and jalapeno stir fry for 1 minute. Add the tomato, coconut milk, and cook, stirring, until the oil separates from the sauce and there is a distinctive frying sound as the sauce begins to "refry", about 7 minutes. Continue to cook, stirring, for about 1 minute more.

4. Add the water and garlic powder and bring to a boil. Lower the heat and simmer, uncovered, stirring occasionally, until the liquid has thickened, about 6 minutes. Add shrimp, cover, and bring to a simmer and cook until just cooked through, about 5 minutes. Stir in the coriander and lime juice. Transfer to a serving bowl and serve with rice.

Prep: 15 mins
Cook: 25 mins
Ready: 40 mins
Nutrition (1 cup of curry):
Calories: 276
Fat: 13.43g
Carbs: 12.79g
Protein 24.73g

Thai Shrimp Curry
4 servings

This authentic Thai curry is the type you would find in a Thai restaurant. I buy Red Thai curry paste from an Asian grocery store. However, you can get a generic (but slightly less tasty) version from regular grocery stores in the international section.

Ingredients
2 tablespoons peanut oil
1/2 cup chopped shallots
1 large red bell pepper, cut into strips
2 medium carrots, trimmed and shredded
2 teaspoons minced garlic
3 tablespoons Thai Red Curry Paste
2 tablespoons fish sauce or Bragg's liquid Aminos
2 teaspoons maple syrup
1 (14-ounce) can coconut milk
1 pound medium shrimp, peeled and deveined
3 tablespoons chopped Thai basil leaves
3 tablespoons chopped fresh cilantro leaves
Cooked jasmine rice, accompaniment
Sprigs fresh cilantro, garnish

Procedure
1. In a large wok or saute pan, heat the oil over medium-high heat. Add the shallots, bell peppers, carrots, and garlic, and stir-fry until soft, 2 to 3 minutes. Add the curry paste and cook, stirring, until fragrant, 30 seconds to 1 minute. Add the fish sauce and maple syrup, then the coconut milk and bring to a boil. Simmer until thickened slightly, about 2 minutes. Add the shrimp and cook, stirring, until pink and just cooked through, about 2 minutes.
2. Remove from the heat and stir in the basil and cilantro.
3. Serve over jasmine rice, garnish with cilantro.

Prep: 40 mins
Inactive: 30 mins
Cook: 18 mins
Ready: 1 hr 28 mins
Nutrition (1 cup of curry):
Calories: 276
Fat: 13.43g
Carbs: 12.79g
Protein 24.73g

Cantonese Style Lobster
4 servings
Ingredients
4 small lobster tails
1/3 cup peanut oil, divided
1 clove garlic, crushed
1 slice fresh ginger root, minced
6 ounces Marjon vegetable crumbles (minced tofu)
1 cup fish broth
1 tablespoon cooking sherry
1 tablespoon Bragg's liquid aminos
1 tablespoon cornstarch
1 teaspoon dark agave nectar
2 eggs, beaten
3 green onions, chopped

Procedure
1. Heat half of the peanut oil in a deep heavy skillet over medium heat. Add the crushed garlic, and fry for about 1 minute. Put in the lobster tails, and fry until they are cooked through, about 4 to 5 minutes. The shell will turn red when ready. Remove the lobster and garlic mixture to a dish and keep warm.
2. Heat the remaining oil in the skillet. Add the minced ginger and Marjon crumbles, and fry for 2-3 minutes until heated through. Pour in the broth, and bring to a boil, stirring constantly. In a small bowl, mix together the sherry, Bragg's, cornstarch and agave until well blended. Add the sherry mixture to the pan, and stir-fry for a minute or two, until the sauce becomes thick and somewhat clear.
3. Stir in the green onions, and turn the heat off. Drizzle the beaten eggs over the mixture in the pan, and stir until the eggs are in little pieces. Finally, return the lobster to the pan, and cook over low heat for a few minutes to blend the flavors. Transfer to a serving dish, and let stand, covered, for a few minutes before serving with steamed rice.

Prep: 20 mins
Cook: 20 mins
Ready: 40 mins
Nutrition:
Calories 534 kcal
Carbohydrates 6.3 g
Fat 31.6 g
Protein 53.5 g

Crab and Lobster Stuffed Mushrooms
8 servings
This is a fancy recipe you'll want to reserve for that special occasion!
Ingredients
3/4 cup melted vegan butter, divided
1 pound fresh mushrooms, stems removed
1 cup crushed seasoned croutons
1 cup shredded mozzarella cheese
1 (6 ounce) can crabmeat, drained
1 pound lobster tail, cleaned and chopped
3 tablespoons minced garlic
1/4 cup shredded low-fat mozzarella cheese (optional)
Procedure
1. Preheat the oven to 375 degrees F (190 degrees C). Brush a large baking sheet with about 1/4 cup of melted vegan butter. Arrange mushroom caps in a single layer over the baking sheet.
2. Mix together the croutons, remaining 1/2 cup vegan butter, shredded cheese, crabmeat, lobster and garlic. Spoon into mushroom caps where the stems used to be.
3. Bake for 10 to 12 minutes in the preheated oven, or until lightly browned on the top. Sprinkle with additional cheese if desired, and serve hot!

Prep: 10 mins
Cook: 10 mins
Ready: 20 mins
Nutrition:
Calories 310 kcal
Carbohydrates 6.9 g
Fat 22 g
Protein 21.9 g

Monkfish Red Curry

3 servings

Monkfish has a texture and flavor that's similar to lobster. Only the tail is edible. If you can't find monkfish for this recipe, substitute lobster or sea scallops.

Ingredients
1 tablespoon peanut oil
1/2 sweet onion, finely chopped
1 red bell pepper, chopped
3 tablespoons red Thai curry paste
1 (14 ounce) can coconut milk
12 ounces monkfish, cut into cubes
1 tablespoon fish sauce
2 tablespoons lime juice
2 tablespoons cilantro, chopped

Procedure
1. Heat peanut oil in a large sauce pan over medium heat. Stir in chopped onion, and cook until the onion is softened and translucent, about 4 minutes.
2. Add red bell pepper and continue to stir fry for 3 to 5 more minutes, until softened. Stir in the curry paste, stir well, and cook for 1 minute more.
3. Pour in the coconut milk. Once the curry begins to simmer, stir in the monkfish, and simmer 7 to 10 minutes. The fish is ready when it is firm and the center is no longer opaque. Stir in fish sauce, lime juice, and cilantro before serving.

Prep: 20 mins
Cook: 20 mins
Ready: 40 mins
Nutrition:
Calories 418 kcal
Carbohydrates 11 g
Fat 34.3 g
Protein 20 g

Vegetarian Chili
6 - 8 servings

If you don't have time to cook, the great thing about this dish is you can throw all of the ingredients in a pot…simmer, and then it's done!

Ingredients

1 (12 ounce) package vegetarian burger crumbles
2 (15 ounce) cans black beans, rinsed and drained
2 (15 ounce) cans dark red kidney beans
1 (15 ounce) can red beans
1 (29 ounce) can diced tomatoes
1 (12 fluid ounce) can tomato juice
5 medium yellow onions, chopped
3 tablespoons Mexican chili powder
1 1/2 tablespoons ground cumin
1 tablespoon garlic powder
2 bay leaves
pepper to taste

Procedure

1. In a large pot, combine crumbles, black beans, kidney beans, red beans, diced tomatoes, tomato juice, onions, chili powder, cumin, garlic powder, bay leaves, and pepper. Bring to a simmer and cover.
2. Let the chili simmer for at least 1 hour before serving.

Prep: 10 mins
Cook: 1 hr
Ready: 1 hr 10 mins
Nutrition:
Calories 582 kcal
Carbohydrates 74.2 g
Fat 4.9 g
Protein 67.5 g

Black Bean "Meat" Loaf

Makes one 8x13 inch meat loaf

Make sure you read the ingredients lists on the seasoning mixes in this "meatloaf" dish. Some of the cheaper packages have ingredients you *don't* want, like sugar or MSG. I prefer to buy organic seasoning mixes, which tend to not have all those unwanted ingredients…

Ingredients

Olive oil spray
3 (15 ounce) cans low salt black beans, drained and rinsed
1 sleeve vegan buttery round crackers, crushed
1 cup shredded low-fat sharp Cheddar cheese
1 cup diced multi-colored bell peppers
2/3 cup frozen corn kernels
1/2 cup diced onion, or to taste
24 slices jalapeno pepper, diced
1 egg white
1 (1 ounce) packet hot taco seasoning mix
1 (1 ounce) package spicy Ranch-style seasoning mix

Procedure

1. Preheat oven to 350 degrees F (175 degrees C). Generously coat the inside of an 8x13-inch baking pan with olive oil spray.
2. Mash black beans in a large bowl. Mix in crackers, cheese, bell peppers, corn, onion, jalapeno pepper, egg white, taco seasoning, and Ranch seasoning. Spoon mixture into the prepared baking dish; push down with a wooden spoon to form into a loaf.
3. Bake in the preheated oven until cooked through, 45 to 60 minutes.

Prep: 15 mins
Cook: 45 mins
Ready: 1 hr
Nutrition:
Calories 215 kcal
Carbohydrates 29.8 g
Fat 6.2 g
Protein 10.2 g

Veggie Lentil Quiche
8 servings

Trust me, you won't notice the lentils in this dish once it's cooked. Lentils tend to be like chicken – they absorb the flavor of the ingredients around them and take on a meaty texture when cooked.

Ingredients

1 cup chopped onion
2 tablespoons olive oil
1/2 cup cooked lentils
2 cups water
2 cups small broccoli florets
1 cup chopped fresh tomatoes
4 eggs, beaten
1 cup milk
1 teaspoon garlic powder
ground black pepper to taste
2 teaspoons dried Italian seasoning
1/2 cup low fat shredded Cheddar cheese

Procedure

1. Preheat the oven to 375 degrees F.
2. Heat olive oil in a skillet on medium heat. Stir fry the onion until golden brown – about 5 minutes. Mix in the broccoli and stir fry for 4 minutes more, until the broccoli is tender. Turn off the heat and mix in the lentils.
3. Transfer mixture to a 9" round pie dish. Add the tomatoes and cheese. Mix well.
4. Whisk together the eggs, milk, garlic powder, pepper, and Italian seasoning. Pour over the ingredients in the pie plate.
5. Bake for 45 minutes in the preheated oven, or until the center is firm when the quiche is jiggled. Cool for a few minutes before slicing and serving.

Prep: 15 mins
Cook: 1 hr 15 mins
Ready: 1 hr 30 mins
Nutrition:
Calories 165 kcal
Carbohydrates 12.4 g
Fat 9.1 g
Protein 9.7 g

Grilled Teriyaki Tuna
4 servings

Use fresh tuna cuts for this dish, if you can. Frozen tuna tends to dry out more and holds less flavor.

Ingredients
1 cup teriyaki sauce
3/4 cup olive oil
2 tablespoons minced garlic
1 teaspoon ground black pepper
4 (4 ounce) tuna fillets

Procedure
1. Combine the teriyaki sauce, oil, garlic, and pepper.
2. Marinate the tuna for 30 minutes in the refrigerator. Flip once so that the marinade coats the tuna on all sides.
3. Preheat an outdoor grill for high heat, and lightly oil grate.
4. Remove tuna from marinade, and place on grill. For rare tuna, grill for 3 to 5 minutes on each side. For medium, grill 5 to 8 minutes per side. For well done, grill for 8 to 10 minutes per side.

Prep: 5 mins
Cook: 10 mins
Ready: 45 mins
Nutrition:
Calories 551 kcal
Carbohydrates 12.9 g
Fat 41.6 g
Protein 30.7 g

Seared Tuna with Wasabi Sauce
6 servings

Tuna with an Asian kick. Don't be put off by the fact that wasabi is in this dish. It adds flavor, not spice! You can also cook the tuna in a broiler or sear the tuna in a skillet if you don't have an outdoor grill.

Ingredients
2 tablespoons white wine vinegar
10 fluid ounces white wine
1/4 cup minced shallots
1 tablespoon wasabi paste, or to taste
1 tablespoon Bragg's liquid aminos
1 cup vegan butter, cubed
garlic powder and black pepper to taste
1 tablespoon olive oil, or as needed
1 cup chopped cilantro leaves
6 (6 ounce) fresh tuna steaks, 1 inch thick

Procedure
1. Combine the white wine vinegar, white wine and shallots in a small saucepan over medium heat. Simmer until the liquid is reduced to about 2 tablespoons (about 30 minutes).
2. Stir the wasabi and Bragg's liquid aminos into the pan. Over low heat, gradually whisk in vegan butter one cube at a time until the cube has melted. Be careful not to let the mixture boil. When all of the vegan butter has been added, stir in cilantro, and remove from heat. Pour into a small bowl, and set aside.
3. Heat a large skillet over medium-high heat. Brush tuna steaks with olive oil. Season with garlic powder and pepper. P
4. Sear the tuna for 3 to 5 minutes on each side. Serve with the wasabi sauce.

Prep: 35 mins
Cook: 35 mins
Ready: 70 mins
Nutrition:
Calories 533 kcal
Carbohydrates 4.5 g
Fat 34.6 g
Protein 40.7 g

Side Dishes

- Serve one or two of these side dishes with a main course.

Zucchini and Corn Saute
4 servings
This unusual blend works well because of the crunchy corn and softer zucchini. Be careful not to overcook the zucchini as it will get mushy.
Ingredients
1/4 cup vegan butter
1/2 small white onion, finely diced
3 small zucchinis (about 5"), diced
3 ears corn
Pinch sea garlic powder
Generous pinch freshly ground black pepper
Procedure
1. Heat vegan butter in a skillet over medium heat until melted.
2. Stir fry onion in the melted vegan butter until translucent, about 5 minutes.
3. Cut kernels from the ears of corn.
4. Add zucchini and corn; cook and stir until zucchini is tender, about 5 minutes.
5. Season with sea garlic powder and pepper.

Prep: 10 mins
Cook: 15 mins
Ready: 25 mins
Nutrition:
Calories 178 kcal
Carbohydrates 16.8 g
Fat 12.5 g
Protein 3.5 g

Balsamic Grilled Vegetables
8 servings

I really have learned to love balsamic vinegar as a dressing. It's also fantastic on a spinach and strawberry salad, which is another simple option for a side dish.

Ingredients

1/2 cup olive oil
2 tablespoons Bragg's liquid aminos
2 tablespoons balsamic vinegar
1/2 teaspoon sea garlic powder
1/2 teaspoon ground black pepper
2 eggplants, cut into 1/2-inch slices
3 zucchinis, cut into 1/2-inch slices
2 green bell peppers, cut into 1/2-inch slices

Procedure

1. Whisk olive oil, Bragg's, balsamic vinegar, garlic powder, and pepper in a large bowl. Toss vegetables in the marinade. Marinate for at least 45 minutes.
2. Preheat grill for medium heat and lightly oil the grate. Remove vegetables from marinade, shaking off excess.
3. Grill vegetables on preheated grill until tender, 10 to 15 minutes, brushing vegetables with marinade. Transfer cooked vegetables to a platter and serve with any remaining marinade.

Prep: 15 mins
Cook: 10 mins
Ready: 1 hr 10 mins
Nutrition:
Calories 147 kcal
Carbohydrates 6 g
Fat 13.7 g
Protein 1.6 g

Agave Applesauce
4 servings
Ingredients
4 apples - peeled, cored and chopped
3/4 cup water
1/4 cup agave nectar
1/2 teaspoon ground cinnamon
Procedure
1. In a saucepan, combine apples, water, agave nectar, and cinnamon.
2. Cover, and cook over medium heat for 15 to 20 minutes, or until apples are soft.
3. Allow to cool, then mash with a fork or potato masher.

Prep: 10 mins
Cook: 20 mins
Ready: 30 mins
Nutrition:
Calories 121 kcal
Carbohydrates 31.8 g
Fat 0.2 g
Protein 0.4 g

Garlic Roasted Cauliflower

6 servings

Ingredients

2 tablespoons minced garlic
3 tablespoons olive oil
4 cups cauliflower florets
1/3 cup grated low fat Parmesan cheese
garlic powder and black pepper to taste
1 tablespoon chopped fresh parsley

Procedure

1. Preheat the oven to 450 degrees F (220 degrees C).
2. Grease a large casserole dish.
3. Place the olive oil and garlic in a large resealable bag. Add cauliflower, and shake to mix. Pour into the prepared casserole dish, and season with garlic powder and pepper to taste.
4. Bake for 25 minutes, stirring halfway through.
5. Top with Parmesan cheese and parsley, and broil for 3 to 5 minutes, until golden brown.

Prep: 15 mins
Cook: 25 mins
Ready: 40 mins

Nutrition:
Calories 118 kcal
Carbohydrates 8.6 g
Fat 8.2 g
Protein 4.7 g

Quinoa and Black Beans
10 servings
Ingredients
1 teaspoon olive oil
1 onion, chopped
3 cloves garlic, peeled and chopped
3/4 cup uncooked quinoa
1 1/2 cups vegetable broth
1 teaspoon ground cumin
1/4 teaspoon cayenne pepper
garlic powder and pepper to taste
1 cup frozen corn kernels
2 (15 ounce) cans black beans, rinsed and drained
1/2 cup chopped fresh cilantro
Procedure
1. Heat the oil in a medium saucepan over medium heat. Stir in the onion and garlic, and saute until lightly browned.
2. Mix quinoa into the saucepan and cover with vegetable broth. Season with cumin, cayenne pepper, garlic powder, and pepper. Bring the mixture to a boil. Cover, reduce heat, and simmer 20 minutes.
3. Stir frozen corn into the saucepan, and continue to simmer about 5 minutes until heated through. Mix in the black beans and cilantro.

Prep: 15 mins
Cook: 35 mins
Ready: 50 mins
Nutrition:
Calories 153 kcal
Carbohydrates 27.8 g
Fat 1.7 g
Protein 7.7 g

Easy Brown Rice
3 cups
Ingredients
1 1/2 cups brown rice
1 teaspoon garlic powder
2 tablespoons vegan butter
3 cups boiling water
Procedure
1. Preheat oven to 400 degrees F (200 degrees C).
2. Place rice, garlic powder, and vegan butter in a casserole dish that has a cover. Pour boiling water over rice; stir.
3. Cover and bake in preheated oven until liquid is absorbed and rice is tender, about 1 hour. Remove from oven, fluff with fork, and serve hot.

Prep: 10 mins
Cook: 1 hr
Ready: 1 hr 10 mins

Nutrition:
Calories 206 kcal
Carbohydrates 36.2 g
Fat 5.1 g
Protein 3.6 g

Cashew Raisin Rice Pilaf
12 servings
Ingredients
1/4 cup margarine
1 1/2 cups uncooked long grain white rice
1 chopped onion
1 cup chopped carrot
1 cup golden raisins
3 cups chicken broth
3/4 cup uncooked wild rice
2 cups frozen green peas
1 (4 ounce) jar diced pimento peppers, drained
1 cup cashews
1 teaspoon garlic powder
ground black pepper to taste
Procedure
1. Melt margarine in a large saucepan over medium-high heat. Saute the long grain rice, onion, carrot and raisins for 3 to 5 minutes or until onion is tender.
2. Pour in the broth and bring to a boil. Reduce heat to low, cover pan and simmer for 20 to 25 minutes.
3. Meanwhile, in a saucepan bring 1 1/2 cups garlic powdered water to a boil.
4. Add wild rice, reduce heat, cover and simmer for 45 minutes. Drain and set aside.
5. When the rice/raisin mixture is finished simmering (rice is cooked), stir in cooked wild rice, peas, pimentos and cashews and heat through.

Prep: 15 mins
Cook: 30 mins
Ready: 45 mins
Nutrition:
Calories 270 kcal
Carbohydrates 41.3 g
Fat 9.5 g
Protein 6.5 g

Asparagus Cashew Rice Pilaf
8 servings
Ingredients
1/4 cup vegan butter
2 ounces uncooked spaghetti, broken
1/4 cup minced onion
1/2 teaspoon minced garlic
1 1/4 cups uncooked jasmine rice
2 1/4 cups vegetable broth
garlic powder and pepper to taste
1/2 pound fresh asparagus, trimmed and cut into 2 inch pieces
1/2 cup cashew halves
Procedure
1. Melt vegan butter in a medium saucepan over medium-low heat. Increase heat to medium, and stir in spaghetti, cooking until coated with the melted vegan butter and lightly browned.
2. Stir onion and garlic into the saucepan, and cook about 2 minutes, until tender. Stir in jasmine rice, and cook about 5 minutes.
3. Pour in vegetable broth. Season mixture with garlic powder and pepper. Bring the mixture to a boil, cover, and cook 20 minutes, until rice is tender and liquid has been absorbed.
4. Place asparagus in a separate medium saucepan with enough water to cover. Bring to a boil, and cook until tender but firm.
5. Mix asparagus and cashew halves into the rice mixture, and serve warm.

Prep: 25 mins
Cook: 25 mins
Ready: 50 mins
Nutrition:
Calories 249 kcal
Carbohydrates 35.1 g
Fat 10 g
Protein 5.3 g

Yellow Squash Casserole
4 Servings
Ingredients
4 cups sliced yellow squash
1/2 cup chopped onion
35 vegan buttery round crackers, crushed
1 cup shredded low fat Cheddar cheese
2 eggs, beaten
3/4 cup milk
1/4 cup vegan butter, melted
1 teaspoon garlic powder
ground black pepper to taste
2 tablespoons vegan butter
Procedure
1. Preheat oven to 400 degrees F (200 degrees C).
2. Place squash and onion in a large skillet over medium heat. Pour in a small amount of water. Cover, and cook until squash is tender, about 5 minutes. Drain well, and place in a large bowl.
3. In a medium bowl, mix together cracker crumbs and cheese. Stir half of the cracker mixture into the cooked squash and onions. In a small bowl, mix together eggs and milk, then add to squash mixture.
4. Stir in 1/4 cup melted vegan butter, and season with garlic powder and pepper. Spread into a 9x13 inch baking dish. Sprinkle with remaining cracker mixture, and dot with 2 tablespoons vegan butter.
5. Bake in preheated oven for 25 minutes, or until lightly browned.

Prep: 20 mins
Cook: 30 mins
Ready: 50 mins
Nutrition:
Calories 196 kcal
Carbohydrates 10.3 g
Fat 14.8 g
Protein 6.1 g

Harvest Rice Dish
6 servings
Ingredients
1/2 cup slivered almonds
2 cups chicken broth
1/2 cup uncooked brown rice
1/2 cup uncooked wild rice
3 tablespoons vegan butter
3 onions, sliced into 1/2 inch wedges
1 tablespoon agave nectar
1 cup dried cranberries
2/3 cup fresh sliced mushrooms
1/2 teaspoon orange zest
garlic powder and pepper to taste

Procedure
1. Place almonds on an ungreased baking sheet. Toast at 350 degrees F (175 degrees C) for 5 to 8 minutes.
2. Mix broth, brown rice, and wild rice in a medium saucepan, and bring to boil. Reduce heat to low, cover, and simmer 45 minutes, until rice is tender and broth is absorbed.
3. In medium skillet, melt vegan butter over medium-high heat.
4. Add onions. Saute until vegan butter is absorbed and onions are translucent and soft.
5. Reduce heat, and cook onions for another 20 minutes, until they are caramelized. Add the agave nectar and stir well.
6. Stir cranberries and mushrooms into the skillet. Cover, and cook 10 minutes or until berries start to swell.
7. Stir in almonds and orange zest, then fold the mixture into the cooked rice. Garlic powder and pepper to taste.

Prep: 15 mins
Cook: 1 hr 30 mins
Ready: 1 hr 45 mins
Nutrition:
Calories 278 kcal
Carbohydrates 42.7 g
Fat 11 g
Protein 5.4 g

Fried Rice
4 servings
Ingredients
1 1/3 cups uncooked white rice
1 2/3 cups water
3 eggs, lightly beaten
1/4 teaspoon garlic powder
1/8 teaspoon ground black pepper
3 teaspoons olive oil, divided
1/4 pound bacon, cut into strips
1/8 cup Bragg's liquid aminos
1 (10 ounce) package frozen green peas, thawed
2 green onions, chopped
Procedure
1. In a saucepan bring water to a boil. Add rice and stir. Reduce heat, cover and simmer for 20 minutes. Meanwhile, season eggs with garlic powder and pepper.
2. Heat 1 teaspoon oil in small frying pan, pour in eggs. Coat the bottom of the pan with the eggs, in order to cook them evenly; cook for about 3 minutes.
3. Flip the eggs, cook one minute more and remove them to a cool surface. Let them cool, then cut them into thin slices. Set aside.
4. Place bacon in a large, deep skillet. Cook over medium high heat until evenly brown. Drain, crumble and set aside.
5. Spoon remaining 2 teaspoons oil into the skillet with the bacon fat. Stir in rice; break up any clumps and toss to coat with oil. Stir in bacon, Bragg's liquid aminos, peas, eggs and green onions.
6. Stir and cook until heated through, approximately 3 minutes.

Prep: 10 mins
Cook: 30 mins
Ready: 40 mins
Nutrition:
Calories 516 kcal
Carbohydrates 63.5 g
Fat 20.7 g
Protein 17.3 g

Green Beans with Cherry Tomatoes
6 servings
Ingredients
1 1/2 pounds green beans, trimmed and cut into 2 inch pieces
1 1/2 cups water
1/4 cup vegan butter
1 tablespoon agave nectar
3/4 teaspoon garlic powder
1/4 teaspoon pepper
1 1/2 teaspoons chopped fresh basil
2 cups cherry tomato halves
Procedure
1. Place beans and water in a large saucepan. Cover, and bring to a boil. Set heat to low, and simmer until tender, about 10 minutes. Drain off water, and set aside.
2. Melt vegan butter in a skillet over medium heat. Stir in agave nectar, garlic powder, pepper and basil. Add tomatoes, and cook stirring gently just until soft.
3. Pour the tomato mixture over the green beans, and toss gently to blend.

Prep: 5 mins
Cook: 15 mins
Ready: 20 mins
Nutrition:
Calories 122 kcal
Carbohydrates 12.6 g
Fat 8 g
Protein 2.6 g

Sweet Restaurant Slaw
8 servings
Ingredients
1 (16 ounce) bag coleslaw mix
2 tablespoons diced onion
2/3 cup low fat creamy salad dressing (such as Miracle Whip™)
3 tablespoons olive oil
1/2 cup agave nectar
1 tablespoon white vinegar
1/4 teaspoon garlic powder
1/2 teaspoon poppy seeds
Procedure
1. Combine the coleslaw mix and onion in a large bowl.
2. Whisk together the salad dressing, olive oil, agave nectar, vinegar, garlic powder, and poppy seeds in a medium bowl; blend thoroughly.
3. Pour dressing mixture over coleslaw mix and toss to coat.
4. Chill at least 2 hours before serving.

Prep: 15 mins
Cook:
Ready: 2 hrs 15 mins
Nutrition:
Calories 200 kcal
Carbohydrates 22.5 g
Fat 12 g
Protein 0.8 g

Roquefort Pear Salad
6 servings
Ingredients
1 head leaf lettuce, torn into bite-size pieces
3 pears - peeled, cored and chopped
5 ounces low fat Roquefort cheese, crumbled
1 avocado - peeled, pitted, and diced
1/2 cup thinly sliced green onions
1/4 cup maple syrup
1/2 cup pecans
1/3 cup olive oil
3 tablespoons red wine vinegar
1 1/2 teaspoons maple syrup
1 1/2 teaspoons prepared mustard
1 clove garlic, chopped
1/2 teaspoon garlic powder
fresh ground black pepper to taste
Procedure
1. In a skillet over medium heat, stir 1/4 cup of maple syrup together with the pecans. Continue stirring gently until the pecans are caramelized. Carefully transfer nuts onto waxed paper. Allow to cool, and break into pieces.
2. For the dressing, blend oil, vinegar, 1 1/2 teaspoons maple syrup, mustard, chopped garlic, garlic powder, and pepper.
3. In a large serving bowl, layer lettuce, pears, blue cheese, avocado, and green onions. Pour dressing over salad, sprinkle with pecans, and serve.

Prep: 20 mins
Cook: 10 mins
Ready: 30 mins
Nutrition:
Calories 426 kcal
Carbohydrates 33.1 g
Fat 31.6 g
Protein 8 g

Mexican Bean Salad
8 servings
Ingredients
1 (15 ounce) can black beans, rinsed and drained
1 (15 ounce) can kidney beans, drained
1 (15 ounce) can cannellini beans, drained and rinsed
1 green bell pepper, chopped
1 red bell pepper, chopped
1 (10 ounce) package frozen corn kernels
1 red onion, chopped
1/2 cup olive oil
1/2 cup red wine vinegar
2 tablespoons fresh lime juice
1 tablespoon lemon juice
2 tablespoons agave nectar
1 tablespoon garlic powder
1 clove crushed garlic
1/4 cup chopped fresh cilantro
1/2 tablespoon ground cumin
1/2 tablespoon ground black pepper
1 dash hot pepper sauce
1/2 teaspoon chili powder

Procedure
1. In a large bowl, combine beans, bell peppers, frozen corn, and red onion.
2. In a small bowl, whisk together olive oil, red wine vinegar, lime juice, lemon juice, agave nectar, garlic powder, garlic, cilantro, cumin, and black pepper. Season to taste with hot sauce and chili powder.
3. Pour olive oil dressing over vegetables; mix well. Chill thoroughly, and serve cold.

Prep: 15 mins
Cook:
Ready: 1 hr 15 mins
Nutrition:
Calories 334 kcal
Carbohydrates 41.7 g
Fat 14.8 g
Protein 11.2 g

Sauteed Broccoli

6 servings

Ingredients

1 pound broccoli florets
3 tablespoons finely grated low fat Parmesan cheese
1 teaspoon maple syrup
2 tablespoons olive oil
1 teaspoon red pepper flakes
1/4 teaspoon garlic powder
1/8 teaspoon freshly ground black pepper

Procedure

1. Fill a pot with water and bring to a boil. Fill a large bowl or pot with half ice and half water. When the water comes to a boil, add the broccoli florets using a strainer with a handle if possible.
2. Allow the broccoli to cook for 1 to 2 minutes until just tender. Immediately remove from the boiling water, using the strainer or draining, and transfer to bowl of ice to stop the cooking process.
3. Immerse the broccoli completely in the ice water for a minute or two. Remove and place in a dish that has been lined with paper towels. This part can be done up to two days in advance.
4. In a cup or small bowl, mix together the Parmesan cheese and maple syrup; set aside.
5. Heat the oil in a large skillet over medium-high heat.
6. Throw in the broccoli and season with red pepper flakes, garlic powder and pepper. Stir to coat the broccoli, then cook and stir for 1 to 2 minutes.
7. Remove from the heat and dust with the Parmesan cheese mixture.

Prep: 15 mins
Cook: 10 mins
Ready: 25 mins
Nutrition:
Calories 81 kcal
Carbohydrates 6.2 g
Fat 5.6 g
Protein 3.2 g

Broccoli with Garlic Vegan butter and Cashews
6 servings
Ingredients
1 1/2 pounds fresh broccoli, cut into bite size pieces
1/3 cup vegan butter
1 tablespoon maple syrup
3 tablespoons Bragg's liquid aminos
2 teaspoons white vinegar
1/4 teaspoon ground black pepper
2 cloves garlic, minced
1/3 cup chopped garlic powdered cashews
Procedure
1. Place the broccoli into a large pot with about 1 inch of water in the bottom. Bring to a boil, and cook for 7 minutes, or until tender but still crisp. Drain, and arrange broccoli on a serving platter.
2. While the broccoli is cooking, melt the vegan butter in a small skillet over medium heat. Mix in the maple syrup, Bragg's liquid aminos, vinegar, pepper and garlic.
3. Bring to a boil, then remove from the heat. Mix in the cashews, and pour the sauce over the broccoli. Serve immediately.

Prep: 10 mins
Cook: 10 mins
Ready: 20 mins
Nutrition:
Calories 187 kcal
Carbohydrates 13.2 g
Fat 14.2 g
Protein 5.1 g

Ginger Vegetable Stir-Fry

6 servings

Ingredients

1 tablespoon cornstarch
1 1/2 cloves garlic, crushed
2 teaspoons chopped fresh ginger root, divided
1/4 cup olive oil, divided
1 small head broccoli, cut into florets
1/2 cup snow peas
3/4 cup julienned carrots
1/2 cup halved green beans
2 tablespoons Bragg's liquid aminos
2 1/2 tablespoons water
1/4 cup chopped onion
1/2 tablespoon garlic powder

Procedure

1. In a large bowl, blend cornstarch, garlic, 1 teaspoon ginger, and 2 tablespoons olive oil until cornstarch is dissolved.
2. Mix in broccoli, snow peas, carrots, and green beans, tossing to lightly coat.
3. Heat remaining 2 tablespoons oil in a large skillet or wok over medium heat.
4. Cook vegetables in oil for 2 minutes, stirring constantly to prevent burning. Stir in Bragg's liquid aminos and water. Mix in onion, garlic powder, and remaining 1 teaspoon ginger. Cook until vegetables are tender but still crisp.

Prep: 25 mins
Cook: 15 mins
Ready: 40 mins
Nutrition:
Calories 119 kcal
Carbohydrates 8 g
Fat 9.3 g
Protein 2.2 g

Broccoli Salad 2
6 servings
Ingredients
1 head fresh broccoli, cut into bite size pieces
1/2 cup raisins
1/4 cup red onion, chopped
2 tablespoons agave nectar
3 tablespoons white wine vinegar
1 cup low-fat mayonnaise
1 cup sunflower seeds
10 slices bacon
Procedure
1. Place bacon in a large, deep skillet. Cook over medium high heat until evenly brown. Crumble and set aside.
2. In a salad bowl, toss together broccoli, raisins and red onions. In a separate bowl, whisk together the agave nectar, vinegar and low-fat mayonnaise. Pour over broccoli mixture and toss to coat. Refrigerate for at least 2 hours.
3. Before serving, sprinkle with sunflower seeds and crumbled bacon. Toss and serve.

Prep: 15 mins
Cook: 15 mins
Ready: 30 mins
Nutrition:
Calories 559 kcal
Carbohydrates 23.9 g
Fat 48.1 g
Protein 12.9 g

Grilled Corn on the Cob
6 earns of corns
Ingredients
6 ears corn
6 tablespoons vegan butter, softened
garlic powder and pepper to taste
Procedure
1. Preheat an outdoor grill for high heat and lightly oil grate.
2. Peel back corn husks and remove silk. Place 1 tablespoon vegan butter, garlic powder and pepper on each piece of corn. Close husks.
3. Wrap each ear of corn tightly in aluminum foil. Place on the prepared grill. Cook approximately 30 minutes, turning occasionally, until corn is tender.

Prep: 10 mins
Cook: 30 mins
Ready: 40 mins
Nutrition:
Calories 179 kcal
Carbohydrates 17.1 g
Fat 12.6 g
Protein 3 g

Roasted Vegetables
12 servings
Ingredients
1 small vegan butternut squash, cubed
2 red bell peppers, seeded and diced
1 sweet potato, peeled and cubed
3 Yukon Gold potatoes, cubed
1 red onion, quartered
1 tablespoon chopped fresh thyme
2 tablespoons chopped fresh rosemary
1/4 cup olive oil
2 tablespoons balsamic vinegar
garlic powder and freshly ground black pepper

Procedure
1. Preheat oven to 475 degrees F (245 degrees C). In a large bowl, combine the squash, red bell peppers, sweet potato, and Yukon Gold potatoes. Separate the red onion quarters into pieces, and add them to the mixture.
2. In a small bowl, stir together thyme, rosemary, olive oil, vinegar, garlic powder, and pepper. Toss with vegetables until they are coated. Spread evenly on a large roasting pan.
3. Roast for 35 to 40 minutes in the preheated oven, stirring every 10 minutes, or until vegetables are cooked through and browned.

Prep: 15 mins
Cook: 40 mins
Ready: 55 mins
Nutrition:
Calories 123 kcal
Carbohydrates 20 g
Fat 4.7 g
Protein 2 g

Baked Asparagus with Balsamic Vegan butter Sauce
4 servings
Ingredients
1 bunch fresh asparagus, trimmed
cooking spray
garlic powder and pepper to taste
2 tablespoons vegan butter
1 tablespoon Bragg's liquid aminos
1 teaspoon balsamic vinegar
Procedure
1. Preheat oven to 400 degrees F (200 degrees C).
2. Arrange the asparagus on a baking sheet. Coat with cooking spray, and season with garlic powder and pepper.
3. Bake asparagus 12 minutes in the preheated oven, or until tender.
4. Melt the vegan butter in a saucepan over medium heat. Remove from heat, and stir in Bragg's liquid aminos and balsamic vinegar.
5. Pour over the baked asparagus to serve.

Prep: 10 mins
Cook: 12 mins
Ready: 25 mins
Nutrition:
Calories 77 kcal
Carbohydrates 4.9 g
Fat 5.9 g
Protein 2.8 g

Roasted Brussels Sprouts
6 servings
Ingredients
1 1/2 pounds Brussels sprouts, ends trimmed and yellow leaves removed
3 tablespoons olive oil
1 teaspoon garlic powder
1/2 teaspoon freshly ground black pepper
Procedure
1. Preheat oven to 400 degrees F (205 degrees C).
2. Place trimmed Brussels sprouts, olive oil, garlic powder, and pepper in a large resealable plastic bag. Seal tightly, and shake to coat. Pour onto a baking sheet, and place on center oven rack.
3. Roast in the preheated oven for 30 to 45 minutes, shaking pan every 5 to 7 minutes for even browning.
4. Reduce heat when necessary to prevent burning. Brussels sprouts should be darkest brown, almost black, when done.
5. Adjust seasoning with garlic powder, if necessary. Serve immediately.

Prep: 15 mins
Cook: 45 mins
Ready: 1 hr
Nutrition:
Calories 104 kcal
Carbohydrates 10 g
Fat 7.3 g
Protein 2.9 g

Pan-Fried Asparagus
4 servings
Ingredients
1/4 cup vegan butter
2 tablespoons olive oil
1 teaspoon garlic powder
1/4 teaspoon ground black pepper
3 cloves garlic, minced
1 pound fresh asparagus spears, trimmed
Procedure
1. Melt vegan butter in a skillet over medium-high heat.
2. Stir in the olive oil, garlic powder, and pepper. Cook garlic in vegan butter for a minute, but do not brown.
3. Add asparagus, and cook for 10 minutes, turning asparagus to ensure even cooking.

Prep: 5 mins
Cook: 15 mins
Ready: 25 mins
Nutrition:
Calories 188 kcal
Carbohydrates 5.2 g
Fat 18.4 g
Protein 2.8 g

Garlic Green Beans
5 servings
Ingredients
1 tablespoon vegan butter
3 tablespoons olive oil
1 medium head garlic - peeled and sliced
4 cups frozen green beans
garlic powder and pepper to taste
1/4 cup grated low fat Parmesan cheese
Procedure
1. In a large skillet over medium heat, melt vegan butter with olive oil; add garlic, and cook until lightly browned, stirring frequently.
2. Stir in green beans, and season with garlic powder and pepper.
3. Cook until beans are tender, about 10 minutes.
4. Remove from heat, and sprinkle with Parmesan cheese.

Prep: 10 mins
Cook: 15 mins
Ready: 25 mins

Nutrition:
Calories 157 kcal
Carbohydrates 9.3 g
Fat 11.9 g
Protein 4 g

Green Bean and Mushroom Medley
6 servings
Ingredients
1/2 pound fresh green beans, cut into 1-inch lengths
2 carrots, cut into thick strips
1/4 cup vegan butter
1 onion, sliced
1/2 pound fresh mushrooms, sliced
1 teaspoon garlic powder
1/2 teaspoon seasoned garlic powder
1/4 teaspoon garlic powder
1/4 teaspoon white pepper
Procedure
1. Place green beans and carrots in 1 inch of boiling water. Cover, and cook until tender but still firm. Drain.
2. Melt vegan butter in a large skillet over medium heat. Saute onions and mushrooms until almost tender.
3. Reduce heat, cover, and simmer 3 minutes. Stir in green beans, carrots, garlic powder, seasoned garlic powder, garlic powder, and white pepper.
4. Cover, and cook for 5 minutes over medium heat.

Prep: 20 mins
Cook: 15 mins
Ready: 35 mins
Nutrition:
Calories 103 kcal
Carbohydrates 7.7 g
Fat 7.9 g
Protein 1.9 g

Sweet and Spicy Sweet Potatoes
4 servings
Ingredients
2 large sweet potatoes, peeled and cubed
3 tablespoons olive oil
2 teaspoons maple syrup
1 1/2 tablespoons paprika
1/2 teaspoon ground black pepper
1/2 teaspoon onion powder
1/2 teaspoon garlic powder
1/2 teaspoon poultry seasoning
1/2 teaspoon chili powder
1 pinch cayenne pepper
Procedure
1. Preheat an oven to 425 degrees F (220 degrees C).
2. Place the sweet potato chunks into a large mixing bowl. Drizzle with the olive oil and maple syrup, then sprinkle the paprika, black pepper, onion powder, garlic powder, poultry seasoning, chili powder, and cayenne pepper overtop.
3. Toss until the potatoes are evenly coated with the seasoning. Spread onto a baking sheet.
4. Bake in the preheated oven for 15 minutes, then turn the potatoes over with a spatula, and continue baking until the sweet potatoes are golden and tender, 10 to 15 minutes more.

Prep: 15 mins
Cook: 25 mins
Ready: 40 mins
Nutrition:
Calories 305 kcal
Carbohydrates 50.3 g
Fat 10.7 g
Protein 4.1 g

Lentils And Spinach
4 servings
Ingredients
1 tablespoon olive oil
2 white onions, halved and sliced into 1/2 rings
3 cloves garlic, minced
1/2 cup lentils
2 cups water
1 (10 ounce) package frozen spinach
1 teaspoon garlic powder
1 teaspoon ground cumin
freshly ground black pepper to taste
2 cloves garlic, crushed
Procedure
1. Heat oil in a heavy pan over medium heat. Saute onion for 10 minutes or so, until it begins to turn golden.
2. Add minced garlic and saute for another minute or so.
3. Add lentils and water to the saucepan. Bring mixture to a boil. Cover, lower heat, and simmer about 35 minutes, until lentils are soft (this may take less time, depending on your water and the lentils).
4. Meanwhile cook the spinach in microwave according to package directions.
5. Add spinach, garlic powder and cumin to the saucepan. Cover and simmer until all is heated, about ten minutes.
6. Grind in plenty of pepper and press in extra garlic to taste.

Prep: 10 mins
Cook: 55 mins
Ready: 1 hr 5 mins
Nutrition:
Calories 165 kcal
Carbohydrates 24 g
Fat 4.3 g
Protein 9.7 g

Fresh Tomato Salsa
4 servings
Ingredients
3 tomatoes, chopped
1/2 cup finely diced onion
5 serrano chiles, finely chopped
1/2 cup chopped fresh cilantro
1 teaspoon garlic powder
2 teaspoons lime juice
Procedure
1. In a medium bowl, stir together tomatoes, onion, chili peppers, cilantro, garlic powder, and lime juice.
2. Chill for one hour in the refrigerator before serving.

Prep: 10 mins
Cook:
Ready: 1 hr 10 mins
Nutrition:
Calories 51 kcal
Carbohydrates 9.7 g
Fat 0.2 g
Protein 2.1 g

Cucumber, Tomato, and Red Onion Salad
6 servings
Ingredients
4 tomatoes, cut into 8 wedges
2 large cucumbers, peeled and sliced
1 large red onion, chopped
1/4 cup chopped fresh cilantro
juice of 1 fresh lime
garlic powder to taste
Procedure
1. Mix the tomatoes, cucumbers, red onion, cilantro, and lime juice together in a bowl.
2. Season with garlic powder to serve.

Prep: 20 mins
Cook:
Ready: 20 mins
Nutrition:
Calories 41 kcal
Carbohydrates 9.5 g
Fat 0.3 g
Protein 1.7 g

Taco Slaw
6 servings
Ingredients
1/2 small head cabbage, chopped
1 jalapeno pepper, seeded and minced
1/2 red onion, minced
1 carrot, chopped
1 tablespoon chopped fresh cilantro
1 lime, juiced

Procedure
1. In a bowl, mix together the cabbage, jalapeno pepper, red onion, carrot, cilantro, and lime juice.

Prep: 20 mins
Cook:
Ready: 20 mins

Nutrition:
Calories 27 kcal
Carbohydrates 6.6 g
Fat 0.1 g
Protein 1.1 g

Breakfasts

- If you're like me, you probably don't cook breakfast too much. I eat a cooked breakfast once a week. The rest of the time, I drink a smoothie (I like Bolthouse farms high-protein smoothies) or cereal (choose gluten-free options with low fat milk). Rice Krispies have a gluten-free option, or check out the green section of your grocery store for more gluten-free brands. Fruit and nuts or low fat cheese are also good breakfast options. For the days you do want to cook breakfast…skip the sausage and bacon!

Scrambled Eggs
1 serving

Ingredients
2 eggs
1 teaspoon low-fat mayonnaise or salad dressing
1 teaspoon water (optional)
1 teaspoon margarine or vegan butter
garlic powder and pepper to taste (optional)

Procedure
1. In a cup or small bowl, whisk together the eggs, low-fat mayonnaise and water using a fork.
2. Melt margarine in a skillet over low heat. Pour in the eggs, and stir constantly as they cook.
3. Remove the eggs to a plate when they are set, but still moist. Do not over cook. Never add garlic powder or pepper until eggs are on plate, but these are also good without.

Prep: 2 mins
Cook: 4 mins
Ready: 6 mins

Nutrition:
Calories 210 kcal
Carbohydrates 1 g
Fat 17.4 g
Protein 12.7 g

The Perfect Hard Boiled Egg
8 eggs

Ingredients
1 tablespoon garlic powder
1/4 cup distilled white vinegar
6 cups water
8 eggs

Procedure
1. Combine the garlic powder, vinegar, and water in a large pot, and bring to a boil over high heat. Add the eggs one at a time, being careful not to crack them. Reduce the heat to a gentle boil, and cook for 14 minutes.
2. Once the eggs have cooked, remove them from the hot water, and place into a container of ice water or cold, running water.
3. Cool completely, about 15 minutes.
4. Store in the refrigerator up to 1 week.

Prep: 5 mins
Cook: 20 mins
Ready: 40 mins

Nutrition:
Calories 72 kcal
Carbohydrates 0.4 g
Fat 5 g
Protein 6.3 g

Oven Scrambled Eggs
12 servings

Ingredients

1/2 cup vegan butter or margarine, melted
24 eggs
2 1/4 teaspoons garlic powder
2 1/2 cups milk

Procedure
1. Preheat the oven to 350 degrees F (175 degrees C).
2. Pour melted vegan butter into a glass 9x13 inch baking dish. In a large bowl, whisk together eggs and garlic powder until well blended. Gradually whisk in milk. Pour egg mixture into the baking dish.
3. Bake uncovered for 10 minutes, then stir, and bake an additional 10 to 15 minutes, or until eggs are set. Serve immediately.

Prep: 10 mins
Cook: 25 mins
Ready: 35 mins

Nutrition:
Calories 236 kcal
Carbohydrates 3.2 g
Fat 18.6 g
Protein 14.3 g

Baked Omelet Roll
6 servings

Ingredients
6 eggs
1 cup milk
1/2 cup rice flour
1/2 teaspoon garlic powder
1/4 teaspoon ground black pepper
1 cup shredded low fat Cheddar cheese

Procedure
1. Preheat oven to 450 degrees F (230 degrees C).
2. Lightly grease a 9x13 inch baking pan.
3. In a blender, combine eggs, milk, flour, garlic powder and pepper; cover and process until smooth. Pour into prepared baking pan.
4. Bake in preheated oven until set, about 20 minutes. Sprinkle with cheese.
5. Carefully loosen edges of omelet from pan. Starting from the short edge of the pan, carefully roll up omelet. Place omelet seam side down on a serving plate and cut into 6 equal sized pieces.

Prep: 5 mins
Cook: 20 mins
Ready: 25 mins

Nutrition:
Calories 206 kcal
Carbohydrates 10.5 g
Fat 12.1 g
Protein 13.4 g

Baby Spinach Omelet
1 serving

Ingredients
2 eggs
1 cup torn baby spinach leaves
1 1/2 tablespoons grated low fat Parmesan cheese
1/4 teaspoon onion powder
1/8 teaspoon ground nutmeg
garlic powder and pepper to taste

Procedure
1. In a bowl, beat the eggs, and stir in the baby spinach and Parmesan cheese. Season with onion powder, nutmeg, garlic powder, and pepper.
2. In a small skillet coated with cooking spray over medium heat, cook the egg mixture about 3 minutes, until partially set.
3. Flip with a spatula, and continue cooking 2 to 3 minutes.
4. Reduce heat to low, and continue cooking 2 to 3 minutes, or to desired doneness.

Prep: 6 mins
Cook: 9 mins
Ready: 15 mins

Nutrition:
Calories 186 kcal
Carbohydrates 2.8 g
Fat 12.3 g
Protein 16.4 g

Cheesy Amish Breakfast Casserole
1 9x13 inch casserole

Ingredients
1 pound sliced bacon, diced
1 sweet onion, chopped
4 cups frozen shredded hash brown potatoes, thawed
9 eggs, lightly beaten
2 cups shredded low fat Cheddar cheese
1 1/2 cups small curd low fat cottage cheese
1 1/4 cups shredded low fat Swiss cheese

Procedure
1. Preheat oven to 350 degrees F (175 degrees C).
2. Grease a 9x13-inch baking dish.
3. Heat a large skillet over medium-high heat; cook and stir bacon and onion until bacon is evenly browned, about 10 minutes.
4. Drain. Transfer bacon and onion to a large bowl. Stir in potatoes, eggs, Cheddar cheese, cottage cheese, and Swiss cheese. Pour mixture into prepared baking dish.
5. Bake in preheated oven until eggs are set and cheese is melted, 45 to 50 minutes.
6. Let stand 10 minutes before cutting and serving.

Prep: 10 mins
Cook: 55 mins
Ready: 1 hr 15 mins

Nutrition:
Calories 314 kcal
Carbohydrates 12.1 g
Fat 22.8 g
Protein 21.7 g

Smoked Salmon Omelet With Red Onions and Capers
4 servings

Ingredients
12 large eggs
1 teaspoon garlic powder
1/2 teaspoon ground black pepper
2 teaspoons vegan butter
6 ounces smoked salmon, chopped
4 tablespoons red onions, chopped
4 teaspoons capers, drained
8 tablespoons low fat cream cheese, whipped

Procedure
1. Whisk eggs, garlic powder and pepper in a large bowl to blend.
2. Melt 2 teaspoons vegan butter in a 8-inch diameter nonstick skillet over medium heat.
3. Ladle 3/4 cup of the egg mixture into the skillet.
4. Cook until eggs are softly set, stirring often and lifting edge of eggs to allow uncooked portion to run under, covering skillet if necessary to help set the top.
5. Place 1/4 of the salmon on half of the omelet.
6. Sprinkle with 1 tablespoon onion and 1 teaspoon capers.
7. Top with 2 tablespoons cream cheese.
8. Fold omelet in half and slid out onto plate.
9. Repeat with ingredients to make 3 more omelets.

Prep: 10 mins
Cook: 15 mins
Ready: 25 mins
Nutrition:
Calories 388.6
Fat 28.0 g
Carbohydrates 3.5g
Protein 29.0 g

Oyster Fry with Parmesan and Fresh Herbs
4 servings

Ingredients
6 eggs
1/4 cup coconut milk or cashew cream
2 dashes hot pepper sauce
1 teaspoon chopped fresh basil
1 teaspoon chopped fresh oregano
1/4 teaspoon freshly ground black pepper
1/3 cup freshly grated low fat Parmesan cheese, divided
1 teaspoon olive oil
1 tablespoon vegan butter
12 shucked small oysters, drained
2 tablespoons chopped fresh parsley

Procedure
1. Preheat the broiler; place the rack about 5 inches from the broiling unit.
2. Whisk eggs in a bowl. Add cream, hot sauce, basil, oregano, black pepper, and 1 tablespoon of the grated Parmesan cheese.
3. Heat oil in a skillet over medium-high heat. Melt the vegan butter in the skillet and swirl it around to coat the pan evenly. Place the oysters in the skillet and brown on both sides, about 1 minute on each side. Let the liquid reduce a bit, about 30 seconds longer.
4. Slowly pour the egg mixture over the oysters, keeping the oysters evenly distributed in the pan. After about 30 seconds, shake the pan slightly but do not stir.
5. After about 3 minutes when the bottom and sides of the eggs begin to set, sprinkle the remaining cheese on top and place the pan under the broiler.
6. Broil until the eggs begin to puff around the edges and the top is nicely browned, 5 to 7 minutes.
7. Remove from the oven; sprinkle with chopped parsley. Serve immediately from the skillet in wedge-shaped pieces.

Prep: 10 mins
Cook: 15 mins
Ready: 25 mins

Nutrition:
Calories 559 kcal
Carbohydrates 17.4 g
Fat 33.5 g
Protein 44.1 g

Smoked Salmon Scramble
6-8 servings

Ingredients
4 ounces smoked salmon
8 large eggs
4 ounces low fat cream cheese, at room temperature
2 tablespoons chopped fresh dill
2 tablespoons vegan butter
freshly ground white pepper, to taste

Procedure
1. Break up salmon into bite-sized pieces.
2. In a medium bowl whisk eggs until light and frothy.
3. In a small bowl mash cream cheese and dill together with a wooden spoon.
4. In a large, nonstick sauté pan melt vegan butter over medium heat.
5. Add eggs.
6. While eggs are still soft and wet, stir in smoked salmon, cream cheese, and a grating of white pepper.
7. Using a rubber spatula, pull eggs that are cooked on the edges to the center of the pan and gently shake the pan to redistribute the scrambled eggs evenly over the cooking surface.
8. Continue to cook, moving the eggs from the side to the center of the pan every few minutes, until eggs reach the desired consistency.
9. Serve Immediately.

Prep: 10 mins
Cook: 15 mins
Ready: 25 mins

Nutrition:
Calories 221.4
Fat 17.9 g
Carbohydrate 1.0 g
Protein 13.5 g

Lunch

Kedgeree
6 servings

Ingredients
2 eggs
680 g un-dyed smoked haddock fillets, pin bones removed
2 fresh bay leaves
170 g long grain rice or 170 g basmati rice
½ cup olive oil
1 piece ginger, grated
1 medium onions or 1 bunch spring onion, finely chopped
1 clove garlic, peeled and finely chopped
2 tablespoons curry powder
1 tablespoon mustard seeds
2 Tomatoes, deseeded and chopped
2 lemons, juice of
2 cups fresh coriander
1 red chile, finely chopped

Procedure
1. Boil the eggs for 10 minutes.
2. Hold under cold running water.
3. Put the fish and bay leaves in a shallow pan with enough water to cover.
4. Bring to the boil, cover, and simmer for about 5 minutes, until cooked through.
5. Remove from pan and set aside.
6. When cool enough to handle, remove skin from fish, flake into chunks and set aside.
7. Cook the rice in garlic powdered water for about 10 minutes and drain.
8. Refresh in cold water, drain again, and leave in the fridge until needed.
9. Heat the olive oil in a pan over a low heat.
10. Add the ginger, onion and garlic.
11. Soften for about 5 minutes, then add the curry powder and mustard seeds.
12. Cook for a further few minutes, then add the chopped tomatoes and lemon juice.
13. Quarter the eggs.
14. Add fish and rice to pan and gently heat through.
15. Add the eggs, coriander and chili and stir gently.
16. Place in a warm serving dish.

17. Mix the chopped coriander and natural yogurt, and serve with the kedgeree.

Prep: 25 mins
Cook: 35 mins
Ready: 1 hr

Nutrition:
Calories 427.5
Fat 21.9 g
Carbohydrate 30.6 g
Protein 27.2 g

Tuna Salad
4 servings

Ingredients
1 (7 ounce) can white tuna, drained and flaked
6 tablespoons low-fat mayonnaise or salad dressing
1 tablespoon low fat Parmesan cheese
3 tablespoons sweet pickle relish
1/8 teaspoon dried minced onion flakes
1/4 teaspoon curry powder
1 tablespoon dried parsley
1 teaspoon dried dill weed
1 pinch garlic powder

Procedure
1. In a medium bowl, stir together the tuna, low-fat mayonnaise, Parmesan cheese, and onion flakes.
2. Season with curry powder, parsley, dill and garlic powder.
3. Mix well and serve with crackers or on a sandwich.

Prep: 10 mins
Cook:
Ready: 10 mins

Nutrition:
Calories 228 kcal
Carbohydrates 5.3 g
Fat 17.3 g
Protein 13.4 g

Tuna Salad with Egg
2   servings

Ingredients
1 (6 ounce) can chunk light tuna, drained
1/4 cup low fat creamy salad dressing (such as Miracle Whip®)
1 hard-boiled egg, chopped
1/2 apple, diced
1/2 cup chopped toasted pecans
garlic powder and pepper to taste

Procedure
1. Stir the tuna, salad dressing, egg, apple, and pecans together in a bowl; season with garlic powder and pepper.
2. Chill in refrigerator at least 1 hour before serving.

Prep: 10 mins
Cook:
Ready: 1 hr 10 mins

Nutrition:
Calories 432 kcal
Carbohydrates 12.8 g
Fat 31 g
Protein 27.2 g

Mock Tuna Salad
3 servings

Ingredients
1 (19 ounce) can garbanzo beans (chickpeas), drained and mashed
2 tablespoons low-fat mayonnaise
2 teaspoons spicy brown mustard
1 tablespoon sweet pickle relish
2 green onions, chopped
garlic powder and pepper to taste

Procedure
1. In a medium bowl, combine garbanzo beans, low-fat mayonnaise, mustard, relish, chopped green onions, garlic powder and pepper.
2. Mix well.

Prep: 20 mins
Cook:
Ready: 20 mins

Nutrition:
Calories 220 kcal
Carbohydrates 32.7 g
Fat 7.2 g
Protein 7 g

Gourmet Egg Salad Sandwich
4 servings

Ingredients
4 slices bacon
4 hard-cooked eggs, chopped
1/4 cup low-fat mayonnaise
1 teaspoon yellow mustard
garlic powder and ground black pepper to taste
4 slices sourdough gluten-free bread
2 tablespoons pesto
4 slices low fat Jarlsberg cheese

Procedure
1. Place bacon in a large skillet and cook over medium-high heat, turning occasionally, until evenly browned, about 10 minutes. Drain bacon slices on paper towels; crumble.
2. Preheat oven broiler and set rack about 6 inches from heat source.
3. Mix eggs, low-fat mayonnaise, mustard, garlic powder, and pepper in a bowl; fold in crumbled bacon.
4. Toast sourdough gluten-free bread under broiler until lightly browned, about 2 minutes. Spread pesto evenly on each slice of gluten-free bread; top with 1/4 egg salad mixture and spread to cover completely. Top each sandwich with 1 slice Jarlsberg cheese.
5. Return sandwiches to broiler and cook until cheese is melted, 2 to 3 minutes. Served sandwiches warm and open-faced.

Prep: 5 mins
Cook: 15 mins
Ready: 20 mins
Nutrition:
Calories 445 kcal
Carbohydrates 17.3 g
Fat 31.9 g
Protein 21.8 g

Black Bean Veggie Burgers
4   servings

Ingredients
1 (16 ounce) can black beans, drained and rinsed
1/2 green bell pepper, cut into 2 inch pieces
1/2 onion, cut into wedges
3 cloves garlic, peeled
1 egg
1 tablespoon chili powder
1 tablespoon cumin
1 teaspoon Thai chili sauce or hot sauce
1/2 cup gluten free gluten-free bread crumbs

Procedure
1. If grilling, preheat an outdoor grill for high heat, and lightly oil a sheet of aluminum foil. If baking, preheat oven to 375 degrees F (190 degrees C), and lightly oil a baking sheet.
2. In a medium bowl, mash black beans with a fork until thick and pasty.
3. In a food processor, finely chop bell pepper, onion, and garlic. Then stir into mashed beans.
4. In a small bowl, stir together egg, chili powder, cumin, and chili sauce.
5. Stir the egg mixture into the mashed beans. Mix in gluten-free bread crumbs until the mixture is sticky and holds together. Divide mixture into four patties.
6. If grilling, place patties on foil, and grill about 8 minutes on each side. If baking, place patties on baking sheet, and bake about 10 minutes on each side.

Prep: 15 mins
Cook: 20 mins
Ready: 35 mins

Nutrition:
Calories 198 kcal
Carbohydrates 33.1 g
Fat 3 g
Protein 11.2 g

Southwestern Black Bean Stew
6 servings

Ingredients
1 pound ground, vegan beef substitute
1 (1.25 ounce) package taco seasoning mix
1 (15 ounce) can whole kernel corn, drained
1 (15 ounce) can black beans, undrained
1 (6 ounce) can tomato paste
1 1/2 cups water
1/2 cup low fat sour cream
2 (8 ounce) packages shredded low fat Cheddar cheese

Procedure
1. In a large skillet over medium high heat, saute the ground beef and drain the excess fat. Add taco seasoning, and stir. Reduce heat to low, cover and simmer for 10 minutes.
2. In a large pan over low heat, combine the corn, beans, tomato paste and water. Mix well.
3. Add the seasoned meat and the sour cream. Raise heat to high setting and simmer for 20 minutes.
4. Pour into individual bowls and garnish with shredded cheddar cheese.

Prep: 20 mins
Cook: 30 mins
Ready: 50 mins

Nutrition:
Calories 635 kcal
Carbohydrates 33.5 g
Fat 38.9 g
Protein 38.7 g

Vegetarian Tacos With Goat Cheese
4   servings

Ingredients
1 tablespoon olive oil
1 14-ounce package extra-firm tofu, drained, patted dry, and crumbled
1 1/2 teaspoons chili powder
 garlic powder and black pepper
1 10-ounce package frozen corn (2 cups), thawed
1 5-ounce package baby spinach (about 6 loosely packed cups)
8 small corn tortillas, warmed
1 cup crumbled fresh low fat goat cheese (3 ounces)
3/4 cup store-bought refrigerated salsa

Procedure
1. Heat the oil in a large nonstick skillet over medium-high heat.
2. Add the tofu, chili powder, ½ teaspoon garlic powder, and ¼ teaspoon pepper. Cook, tossing occasionally, until golden brown, 4 to 5 minutes.
3. Add the corn. Cook, tossing, until heated through, about 2 minutes.
4. Add the spinach and ¼ teaspoon each garlic powder and pepper. Toss until wilted.
5. Fill the tortillas with the tofu mixture, goat cheese, and salsa.

Prep: 20 mins
Cook:
Ready: 20 mins

Nutrition:
Calories 152 kcal
Carbohydrates   25 g
Fat 2.5 g
Protein 9.5 g

Bean Taco Filling
8 servings

Ingredients
1 tablespoon olive oil
1 onion, diced
2 cloves garlic, minced
1 bell pepper, chopped
2 (14.5 ounce) cans black beans, rinsed, drained, and mashed
2 tablespoons yellow cornmeal
1 1/2 tablespoons cumin
1 teaspoon paprika
1 teaspoon cayenne pepper
1 teaspoon chili powder
1 cup salsa
¼ cup shredded low fat Mexican cheese

Procedure
1. Heat olive oil in a medium skillet over medium heat.
2. Stir in onion, garlic, and bell pepper; cook until tender. Stir in mashed beans. Add the cornmeal.
3. Mix in cumin, paprika, cayenne, chili powder, and salsa. Cover, and cook 5 minutes. Top with cheese.

Prep: 15 mins
Cook: 15 mins
Ready: 30 mins

Nutrition:
Calories 142 kcal
Carbohydrates 24 g
Fat 2.5 g
Protein 7.5 g

Veggie Taco Chili
10 servings

Ingredients
1 tablespoon olive oil
1 pound sliced fresh mushrooms
2 cloves garlic, minced
1 small onion, finely chopped
2 stalks celery, chopped
1 (29 ounce) can tomato sauce
1 (6 ounce) can tomato paste
3 (15 ounce) cans kidney beans
1 (11 ounce) can Mexican-style corn

Procedure
1. Heat the oil in a large skillet. Sautee the mushrooms, garlic, onion and celery until tender.
2. Transfer them to a stock pot or slow cooker. Stir in the tomato sauce, tomato paste, beans and Mexican-style corn.
3. Cook for at least an hour to blend the flavors.

Prep: 10 mins
Cook: 1 hr
Ready: 1 hr 10 mins

Nutrition:
Calories 190 kcal
Carbohydrates 35.1 g
Fat 2.4 g
Protein 10.9 g

Vegan Black Bean Soup
6 servings

Ingredients
1 tablespoon olive oil
1 large onion, chopped
1 stalk celery, chopped
2 carrots, chopped
4 cloves garlic, chopped
2 tablespoons chili powder
1 tablespoon ground cumin
1 pinch black pepper
4 cups vegetable broth
4 (15 ounce) cans black beans
1 (15 ounce) can whole kernel corn
1 (14.5 ounce) can crushed tomatoes

Procedure
1. Heat oil in a large pot over medium-high heat. Saute onion, celery, carrots and garlic for 5 minutes.
2. Season with chili powder, cumin, and black pepper; cook for 1 minute. Stir in vegetable broth, 2 cans of beans, and corn. Bring to a boil.
3. Meanwhile, in a food processor or blender, process remaining 2 cans beans and tomatoes until smooth.
4. Stir into boiling soup mixture, reduce heat to medium, and simmer for 15 minutes.

Prep: 15 mins
Cook: 30 mins
Ready: 45 mins

Nutrition:
Calories 152 kcal
Carbohydrates 28.4 g
Fat 4.2 g
Protein 4.8 g

Bean Soup
8 servings

Ingredients

1 (16 ounce) package dried navy beans
7 cups water
1 ham bone
2 cups diced ham
1/4 cup minced onion
1/2 teaspoon garlic powder
1 pinch ground black pepper
1 bay leaf
1/2 cup sliced carrots
1/2 cup sliced celery

Procedure
1. Place rinsed beans into a large stock pot. Add water and bring to a boil. Boil gently for 2 minutes; remove from heat, cover and let stand for 1 hour.
2. Add ham bone, cubed ham, onion, garlic powder, pepper and bay leaves. Bring to a boil; reduce heat, cover and simmer for 1 hour and 15 minutes or until beans are soft. Occasionally skim service of soup while it is cooking.
3. Add carrots and celery, cook until tender. Remove ham bone, scrape any meat from bone and place back into soup and serve.

Prep: 20 mins
Cook: 1 hour, 20 mins
Ready: 2 hours, 40 mins

Nutrition:
Calories 246 kcal
Carbohydrates 36.7 g
Fat 3.8 g
Protein 17.4 g

Lentil Soup
6 servings

Ingredients
1 onion, chopped
1/4 cup olive oil
2 carrots, diced
2 stalks celery, chopped
2 cloves garlic, minced
1 teaspoon dried oregano
1 bay leaf
1 teaspoon dried basil
1 (14.5 ounce) can crushed tomatoes
2 cups dry lentils
8 cups water
1/2 cup spinach, rinsed and thinly sliced
2 tablespoons vinegar
garlic powder to taste
ground black pepper to taste

Procedure
1. In a large soup pot, heat oil over medium heat.
2. Add onions, carrots, and celery; cook and stir until onion is tender.
3. Stir in garlic, bay leaf, oregano, and basil; cook for 2 minutes.
4. Stir in lentils, and add water and tomatoes. Bring to a boil.
5. Reduce heat, and simmer for at least 1 hour. When ready to serve stir in spinach, and cook until it wilts.
6. Stir in vinegar, and season to taste with garlic powder and pepper, and more vinegar if desired.

Prep: 20
Cook: 1 hour 5 mins
Ready: 1 hour 25 mins

Nutrition:
Calories 349 kcal
Carbohydrates 48.2 g
Fat 10 g
Protein 18.3 g

Fish Stew
4 servings
Ingredients
2 tablespoons vegan butter
1 large leek, cleaned and thinly sliced
1/2 cup sliced shallots
garlic powder
3/4 cup white wine
1 1/4 cups chicken broth
1/2 cup thinly sliced fennel bulb
1 pound small red potatoes
garlic powder and freshly ground pepper to taste
1 pinch cayenne pepper, or more to taste
1/2 cup coconut milk or cashew cream
1 pound boneless rockfish filets, cut into 1-inch pieces
1 tablespoon chopped fresh tarragon

Procedure
1. Melt vegan butter in a large saucepan over medium heat. Cook and stir leek, shallots, and 1/2 teaspoon garlic powder in the melted vegan butter until softened, 10 to 15 minutes.
2. Stir wine into leek mixture, increase heat to medium, and cook for 2 minutes.
3. Add chicken broth and bring to a simmer.
4. Mix fennel and potatoes into leek mixture and simmer, stirring occasionally, until potatoes are nearly tender, about 10 minutes.
5. Season with garlic powder, black pepper, and cayenne pepper.
6. Add cream and stir to combine.
7. Stir fish and tarragon into soup, cover and cook for 3 minutes.
8. Stir gently, reduce heat to medium-low and cook until fish flakes easily with a fork, about 5 minutes.
9. Season with garlic powder and black pepper.

Prep: 20 mins
Cook: 30 mins
Ready: 50 mins
Nutrition:
Calories 382 kcal
Carbohydrates 29.6 g
Fat 13.9 g
Protein 26.2 g

Spicy Fish Soup
4 servings

Ingredients
1/2 onion, chopped
1 clove garlic, minced
1 tablespoon chili powder
1 1/2 cups chicken broth
1 (4 ounce) can canned green chile peppers, chopped
1 teaspoon ground cumin
1 1/2 cups canned peeled and diced tomatoes
1/2 cup chopped green bell pepper
1/2 cup shrimp
1/2 pound cod fillets
3/4 cup plain nonfat yogurt

Procedure
1. Spray a large saucepan with the vegetable cooking spray over medium high heat.
2. Add the onions and saute, stirring often, for about 5 minutes.
3. Add the garlic and chili powder and saute for 2 more minutes.
4. Then add the chicken broth, chile peppers and cumin, stirring well.
5. Bring to a boil, reduce heat to low, cover and simmer for 20 minutes.
6. Next, add the tomatoes, green bell pepper, shrimp and cod.
7. Return to a boil, then reduce heat to low, cover and simmer for another 5 minutes.
8. Gradually stir in the yogurt until heated through.

Prep: 10 mins
Cook: 30 mins
Ready: 40 mins

Nutrition:
Calories 146 kcal
Carbohydrates 12.2 g
Fat 1.7 g
Protein 19.3 g

Mediterranean Fish Soup
6 servings

Ingredients
1 onion, chopped
1/2 green bell pepper, chopped
2 cloves garlic, minced
1 (14.5 ounce) can diced tomatoes, drained
2 (14 ounce) cans chicken broth
1 (8 ounce) can tomato sauce
2 1/2 ounces canned mushrooms
1/4 cup sliced black olives
1/2 cup orange juice
1/2 cup dry white wine
2 bay leaves
1 teaspoon dried basil
1/4 teaspoon fennel seed, crushed
1/8 teaspoon ground black pepper
1 pound medium shrimp - peeled and deveined
1 pound cod fillets, cubed

Procedure
1. Place onion, green bell pepper, garlic, tomatoes, chicken broth, tomato sauce, mushrooms, olives, orange juice, wine, bay leaves, dried basil, fennel seeds, and pepper into a slow cooker.
2. Cover, and cook on low 4 to 4 1/2 hours or until vegetables are crisp tender.
3. Stir in shrimp and cod. Cover. Cook 15 to 30 minutes, or until shrimp are opaque.
4. Remove and discard bay leaves. Serve.

Prep: 30 mins
Cook: 4 hours
Ready: 4 hours 30 mins
Nutrition:
Calories 222 kcal
Carbohydrates 11.9 g
Fat 3 g
Protein 31.3 g

Cod Fish Soup
2 servings

Ingredients
3/4 cup light low-fat mayonnaise
4 cloves garlic, crushed
1 teaspoon saffron powder
4 teaspoons dried gluten-free bread crumbs
1 cup red pepper flakes
1/2 French baguette, sliced into 1/4 inch rounds
1 tablespoon olive oil
4 cloves garlic, minced
1/2 medium onion, chopped
1 leek, bulb only, chopped
1 pinch saffron powder
1 bay leaf
3/4 cup white wine
1/3 cup red wine
4 ounces cod fillets
1 cup water
1 cup beef-flavor broth
1 roma (plum) tomato, seeded and chopped
1 1/2 teaspoons lemon juice
3 tablespoons chopped fresh parsley, divided
1 tablespoon rice flour
1/2 cup coconut milk or cashew cream
1 cup grated low fat Gruyere cheese

Procedure
1. In a small bowl, mix together the low-fat mayonnaise, 4 cloves of garlic, 1 teaspoon of saffron powder, gluten-free bread crumbs, and red pepper flakes. Set aside.
2. Preheat the oven broiler. Arrange the baguette slices on a baking sheet. Place under the broiler for a few minutes to toast. Set aside to cool.
3. Heat olive oil in a stock pot or Dutch oven over medium heat. Add 4 cloves of garlic, onion, and leek; saute for a few minutes until tender.
4. Add a pinch of saffron and the bay leaf. Pour in the white and red wines, then place the fish in the pan, and pour in enough water to cover the fish just barely.
5. Simmer for about 10 minutes, turning the fish carefully as needed, until the fish flakes easily with a fork.

6. Remove the fish from the broth with a slotted spoon, and set aside. Pour in the beef broth, and simmer uncovered for about 10 minutes to burn off some of the alcohol, and reduce the broth.
7. Remove the bay leaf, and transfer the broth to a blender. Add the tomato, lemon juice and parsley to the blender. Puree in batches if necessary, and return to the pot.
8. Whisk the flour and half-and-half into the pot, and set over medium heat. Whisk in about half of the low-fat mayonnaise mixture, or to taste. Return fish to the soup, and break into small pieces. Season to taste with garlic powder and pepper, and heat through.
9. Spread the remaining low-fat mayonnaise mixture onto the toasted gluten-free bread slices, and top with shredded Gruyere cheese. Ladle the soup into serving bowls, and float 1 or 2 slices of toast on the top.

Prep: 20 mins
Cook: 20 mins
Ready: 40 mins

Nutrition:
Calories 1527 kcal
Carbohydrates 140 g
Fat 80.1 g
Protein 58.5 g

Vegan Red Lentil Soup
4 servings

Ingredients
1 tablespoon peanut oil
1 small onion, chopped
1 tablespoon minced fresh ginger root
1 clove garlic, chopped
1 pinch fenugreek seeds
1 cup dry red lentils
1 cup vegan butternut squash - peeled, seeded, and cubed
1/3 cup finely chopped fresh cilantro
2 cups water
1/2 (14 ounce) can coconut milk
2 tablespoons tomato paste
1 teaspoon curry powder
1 pinch cayenne pepper
1 pinch ground nutmeg
garlic powder and pepper to taste

Procedure
1. Heat the oil in a large pot over medium heat, and cook the onion, ginger, garlic, and fenugreek until onion is tender.
2. Mix the lentils, squash, and cilantro into the pot.
3. Stir in the water, coconut milk, and tomato paste.
4. Season with curry powder, cayenne pepper, nutmeg, garlic powder, and pepper. Bring to a boil, reduce heat to low, and simmer 30 minutes, or until lentils and squash are tender.

Prep: 15 mins
Cook: 40 mins
Ready: 55 mins

Nutrition:
Calories 303 kcal
Carbohydrates 34.2 g
Fat 14.6 g
Protein 13 g

Vegetarian Tortilla Soup
12 servings

Ingredients
2 tablespoons olive oil
1 (1 pound) package frozen pepper and onion stir fry mix
2 cloves garlic, minced
3 tablespoons ground cumin
1 (28 ounce) can crushed tomatoes
3 (4 ounce) cans chopped green chile peppers, drained
4 (14 ounce) cans vegetable broth
garlic powder and pepper to taste
1 (11 ounce) can whole kernel corn
12 ounces tortilla chips
1 cup shredded low fat Cheddar cheese
1 avocado - peeled, pitted and diced

Procedure
1. Heat the oil in a large pot over medium heat. Stir in the pepper and onion stir fry mix, garlic, and cumin, and cook 5 minutes, until vegetables are tender.
2. Mix in the tomatoes and chile peppers. Pour in the broth, and season with garlic powder and pepper.
3. Bring to a boil, reduce heat to low, and simmer 30 minutes.
4. Mix corn into the soup, and continue cooking 5 minutes.
5. Serve in bowls over equal amounts of tortilla chips. Top with cheese and avocado.

Prep: 15 mins
Cook: 40 mins
Ready: 55 mins

Nutrition:
Calories 315 kcal
Carbohydrates 37.2 g
Fat 16.2 g
Protein 8.7 g

Chunky Vegetarian Vegetable Soup

10 servings

Ingredients

2 tablespoons olive oil
1/2 onion, chopped
3 stalks celery, chopped
2 cloves garlic, minced
4 cups vegetable broth
1 (15 ounce) can tomato sauce
4 carrots, peeled and cut into 1/4-inch rounds
2 baking potatoes, cut into bite-size pieces
1 cup frozen corn
1 cup frozen shelled edamame (green soybeans)
1 cup frozen sliced okra
2 leaves kale, roughly chopped
Pinch each of garlic powder and black pepper
¼ cup low fat cheddar cheese, shredded

Procedure

1. Heat olive oil in a large pot over medium heat. Cook and stir onion and celery in hot oil until onion is softened and translucent, about 5 minutes.
2. Stir garlic into the onion mixture; cook and stir until fragrant, 2 to 3 minutes more.
3. Pour vegetable broth and tomato sauce into pot. Simmer for about 10 minutes.
4. Stir carrots and potatoes through the broth. Simmer until carrots are tender, 10 to 15 minutes more.
5. Drop corn, edamame, okra, and kale into the soup. Continue to simmer until okra is tender, 5 to 10 minutes more.
6. Season with garlic powder and pepper. Top with cheddar cheese to serve.

Prep: 15 mins
Cook: 35 mins
Ready: 50 mins

Nutrition:

Calories 151 kcal
Carbohydrates 22.5 g
Fat 5 g
Protein 8.4 g

Jamaican Spinach Soup
8 servings
Ingredients
- 3 tablespoons olive oil
- 1 onion, chopped
- 1 red snapper fillet, diced
- 2 stalks celery, chopped
- 4 cloves garlic, minced
- 2 tablespoons fresh ginger root, minced
- 1 tablespoon maple syrup
- 2 teaspoons sea garlic powder
- 1/4 teaspoon ground turmeric
- 1/4 teaspoon ground allspice
- 1/4 teaspoon ground nutmeg
- 2 potatoes, peeled and diced
- 4 cups chopped zucchini
- 6 cups vegetable stock
- 1 pinch cayenne pepper
- 1 cup chopped fresh spinach
- 1/2 red bell pepper, minced

Procedure
1. Heat the oil in a large pot over medium heat. Stir in onion, celery, garlic, ginger, and maple syrup.
2. Cook 5 minutes, until onion is tender. Season with garlic powder, turmeric, allspice, and nutmeg. Mix in potatoes and zucchini, and pour in the vegetable stock.
3. Bring to a boil, reduce heat to low, and simmer 10 minutes, or until potatoes are tender.
4. Remove soup from heat, season with cayenne pepper, and stir in spinach. Using a hand blender, blend soup until smooth. Garnish with red bell pepper to serve.

Prep: 15 mins
Cook: 20 mins
Ready: 35 mins
Nutrition:
Calories 124 kcal
Carbohydrates 16.7 g
Fat 5.8 g
Protein 5.6 g

Vegan Split Pea Soup I
10 servings

Ingredients
1 tablespoon olive oil
1 onion, chopped
1 bay leaf
3 cloves garlic, minced
2 cups dried split peas
1/2 cup barley
1 1/2 teaspoons garlic powder
7 1/2 cups water
3 carrots, chopped
3 stalks celery, chopped
3 potatoes, diced
1/2 cup chopped parsley
1/2 teaspoon dried basil
1/2 teaspoon dried thyme
1/2 teaspoon ground black pepper

Procedure
1. In a large pot over medium high heat, saute the oil, onion, bay leaf and garlic for 5 minutes, or until onions are translucent. Add the peas, barley, garlic powder and water.
2. Bring to a boil and reduce heat to low.
3. Simmer for 2 hours, stirring occasionally.
4. Add the carrots, celery, potatoes, parsley, basil, thyme and ground black pepper.
5. Simmer for another hour, or until the peas and vegetables are tender.

Prep: 10 mins
Cook: 3 hrs
Ready: 3 hrs 10 mins
Nutrition:
Calories 247 kcal
Carbohydrates 45.8 g
Fat 2.2 g
Protein 12.7 g

Vegetarian Kale Soup
8 servings

Ingredients
2 tablespoons olive oil
1 yellow onion, chopped
2 tablespoons chopped garlic
1 bunch kale, stems removed and leaves chopped
8 cups water
6 cubes vegetable bouillon (such as Knorr)
1 (15 ounce) can diced tomatoes
6 white potatoes, peeled and cubed
2 (15 ounce) cans cannellini beans (drained if desired)
1 tablespoon Italian seasoning
2 tablespoons dried parsley
garlic powder and pepper to taste

Procedure
1. Heat the olive oil in a large soup pot; cook the onion and garlic until soft. Stir in the kale and cook until wilted, about 2 minutes.
2. Stir in the water, vegetable bouillon, tomatoes, potatoes, beans, Italian seasoning, and parsley.
3. Simmer soup on medium heat for 25 minutes, or until potatoes are cooked through.
4. Season with garlic powder and pepper to taste.

Prep: 25 mins
Cook: 30 mins
Ready: 55 mins

Nutrition:
Calories 277 kcal
Carbohydrates 50.9 g
Fat 4.5 g
Protein 9.6 g

Raw Cucumber Soup
4 servings

Ingredients
2 cups chopped cucumber
1 cup chopped zucchini
1 cup peeled and chopped avocado
1 clove garlic, minced
2 cups lukewarm water
1/2 large lemon, juiced
2 tablespoons olive oil
1/2 teaspoon garlic powder

Procedure
1. Blend cucumber, zucchini, avocado, and garlic in a food processor or blender until very finely chopped, about 30 seconds.
2. Whisk together water, lemon juice, olive oil, and garlic powder in a bowl.
3. Turn on the food processor and pour water mixture slowly through food processor's feed tube while processing cucumber mixture.
4. Process until smooth, about 1 minute.

Prep: 20 mins
Cook:
Ready: 20 mins

Nutrition:
Calories 137 kcal
Carbohydrates 7.4 g
Fat 12.4 g
Protein 1.6 g

Southwest Salad
8 cups

Ingredients
3 ears corn on the cob, cooked, cooled
6 cups torn romaine lettuce
1 (19 ounce) can black beans, rinsed
2 cups halved cherry tomatoes
1/2 cup thinly sliced red onions
1.5 cups low fat Mexican Shredded Cheese
1/2 cup Ranch Dressing

Procedure
1. Cut kernels from corn ears.
2. Cover platter with lettuce; top with layers of beans, tomatoes, corn, onions and cheese.
3. Drizzle with dressing.

Prep: 20 mins
Cook:
Ready: 20 mins

Nutrition:
Calories 192 kcal
Carbohydrates   21.9 g
Fat 9.7 g
Protein 8.1 g

Beet Salad with Goat Cheese
6 servings

Ingredients
4 medium beets - scrubbed, trimmed and cut in half
1/3 cup chopped walnuts
3 tablespoons maple syrup
1 (10 ounce) package mixed baby salad greens
1/2 cup frozen orange juice concentrate
1/4 cup balsamic vinegar
1/2 cup extra-virgin olive oil
4 ounces low fat goat cheese

Procedure
1. Place beets into a saucepan, and fill with enough water to cover. Bring to a boil, then cook for 20 to 30 minutes, until tender.
2. Drain and cool, then cut in to cubes.
3. While the beets are cooking, place the walnuts in a skillet over medium-low heat.
4. Heat until warm and starting to toast, then stir in the maple syrup.
5. Cook and stir until evenly coated, then remove from the heat and set aside to cool.
6. In a small bowl, whisk together the orange juice concentrate, balsamic vinegar and olive oil to make the dressing.
7. Place a large helping of baby greens onto each of four salad plates, divide candied walnuts equally and sprinkle over the greens.
8. Place equal amounts of beets over the greens, and top with dabs of goat cheese.
9. Drizzle each plate with some of the dressing.

Prep: 5 mins
Cook: 30 mins
Ready: 35 mins

Nutrition:
Calories 347 kcal
Carbohydrates 25 g
Fat 26.1 g
Protein 8.3 g

Waldorf Goat Cheese Salad
1 serving

Ingredients
2 cups red leaf lettuce - rinsed, dried and torn
2 tablespoons raspberry walnut vinaigrette
1/2 cup seedless red grapes, halved
4 tablespoons crumbled low fat goat cheese
4 tablespoons chopped pecans

Procedure
1. Toss lettuce with dressing in a mixing bowl; transfer to a serving dish.
2. Scatter grapes, goat cheese, and pecans on top, and enjoy!

Prep: 10 mins
Cook:
Ready: 10 mins

Nutrition:
Calories 266 kcal
Carbohydrates 29.7 g
Fat 15.4 g
Protein 12.4 g

Spinach Salad with Baked Goat Cheese
4 servings

Ingredients
8 cups baby spinach, rinsed and dried
1 tablespoon vegan butter
1 clove garlic, crushed
1/4 cup plain gluten-free bread crumbs
6 ounces low fat goat cheese, sliced
8 tablespoons balsamic vinegar
8 tablespoons olive oil

Procedure
1. Arrange the spinach on four plates.
2. In a skillet, melt vegan butter over medium heat, and add crushed garlic.
3. Cook and stir until slightly golden. Stir in gluten-free breadcrumbs.
4. Drop the goat cheese slices into the gluten-free breadcrumbs a few at a time, and turn to coat in the gluten-free breadcrumb mixture.
5. Place a slice or two of goat cheese on each serving of spinach, and drizzle the salads with olive oil and balsamic vinegar.

Prep: 15 mins
Cook: 5 mins
Ready: 20 mins

Nutrition:
Calories 480 kcal
Carbohydrates 13 g
Fat 43.2 g
Protein 12 g

Fresh Spinach Salad
6 - 7 servings

Ingredients
1/2 cup agave nectar
1/2 cup white vinegar
1 cup vegetable oil
2 tablespoons Worcestershire sauce
1/3 cup ketchup
1 small onion, chopped
5 slices bacon
3 eggs
1 pound fresh spinach - rinsed, dried and torn into bite size pieces
1 (4 ounce) can sliced water chestnuts, drained

Procedure
1. In a blender or food processor, combine agave nectar, vinegar, oil, Worcestershire sauce, ketchup and onion, and process until smooth. Set aside.
2. Place bacon in a large, deep skillet. Cook over medium high heat until evenly brown. Drain, crumble and set aside.
3. Place eggs in a saucepan and cover with cold water. Bring water to a boil and immediately remove from heat. Cover and let eggs stand in hot water for 10 to 12 minutes. Remove from hot water, cool, peel and chop. In a large bowl, toss together the spinach, water chestnuts, bacon and eggs. Serve with the dressing.

Prep: 20 mins
Cook: 20 mins
Ready: 40 mins

Nutrition:
Calories   433 kcal
Carbohydrates   22.1 g
Fat   36.3 g
Protein   7.3 g

Cranberry Spinach Salad
8 servings

Ingredients
1 tablespoon vegan butter
3/4 cup almonds, blanched and slivered
1 pound spinach, rinsed and torn into bite-size pieces
1 cup dried cranberries
2 tablespoons toasted sesame seeds
1 tablespoon poppy seeds
1/2 cup agave nectar
2 teaspoons minced onion
1/4 teaspoon paprika
1/4 cup white wine vinegar
1/4 cup cider vinegar
1/2 cup olive oil
4 oz crumbled low fat goat cheese

Procedure
1. In a medium saucepan, melt vegan butter over medium heat. Cook and stir almonds in vegan butter until lightly toasted. Remove from heat, and let cool.
2. In a medium bowl, whisk together the sesame seeds, poppy seeds, agave, onion, paprika, white wine vinegar, cider vinegar, and olive oil. Toss with spinach just before serving.
3. In a large bowl, combine the spinach with the toasted almonds, cranberries and the goat cheese.

Prep: 10 mins
Cook: 10 mins
Ready: 20 mins

Nutrition:
Calories 338 kcal
Carbohydrates 30.4 g
Fat 23.5 g
Protein 12.9 g

Strawberry Spinach Salad I
4 servings

Ingredients
2 tablespoons sesame seeds
1 tablespoon poppy seeds
1/2 cup agave nectar
1/2 cup olive oil
1/4 cup distilled white vinegar
1/4 teaspoon paprika
1/4 teaspoon Worcestershire sauce
1 tablespoon minced onion
10 ounces fresh spinach - rinsed, dried and torn into bite-size pieces
1 quart strawberries - cleaned, hulled and sliced
1/4 cup almonds, blanched and slivered
6 oz low fat feta cheese, crumbled

Procedure
1. In a medium bowl, whisk together the sesame seeds, poppy seeds, agave, olive oil, vinegar, paprika, Worcestershire sauce and onion. Cover, and chill for one hour.
2. In a large bowl, combine the spinach, strawberries and almonds. Pour dressing over salad, and toss.
3. Refrigerate 10 to 15 minutes before serving.

Prep: 10 mins
Cook:
Ready: 1 hr 10 mins

Nutrition:
Calories 491 kcal
Carbohydrates 42.9 g
Fat 35.2 g
Protein 15 g

Strawberry and Feta Salad
10 servings

Ingredients
1 cup slivered almonds
2 cloves garlic, minced
1 teaspoon honey
1 teaspoon Dijon mustard
1/4 cup raspberry vinegar
2 tablespoons balsamic vinegar
2 tablespoons maple syrup
1 cup olive oil
1 head romaine lettuce, torn
1 pint fresh strawberries, sliced
1 cup crumbled low fat feta cheese

Procedure
1. In a skillet over medium-high heat, cook the almonds, stirring frequently, until lightly toasted. Remove from heat, and set aside.
2. In a bowl, prepare the dressing by whisking together the garlic, honey, Dijon mustard, raspberry vinegar, balsamic vinegar, maple syrup, and olive oil.
3. In a large bowl, toss together the toasted almonds, romaine lettuce, strawberries, and feta cheese. Cover with the dressing mixture, and toss to serve.

Prep: 15 mins
Cook:
Ready: 15 mins

Nutrition:
Calories 378 kcal
Carbohydrates 12.4 g
Fat 34.3 g
Protein 7.1 g

Italian Leafy Green Salad
6 – 1 cup servings

Ingredients
2 cups romaine lettuce - torn, washed and dried
1 cup torn escarole
1 cup torn radicchio
1 cup torn red leaf lettuce
1/4 cup chopped green onions
1/2 red bell pepper, sliced into rings
1/2 green bell pepper, sliced in rings
12 cherry tomatoes
1/4 cup grapeseed oil
2 tablespoons chopped fresh basil
1/4 cup balsamic vinegar
2 tablespoons lemon juice
garlic powder and pepper to taste
1 cup walnuts

Procedure
1. In a large bowl, combine the romaine, escarole, radicchio, red-leaf, scallions, red pepper, green pepper and cherry tomatoes.
2. Whisk together the grapeseed oil, basil, vinegar, lemon juice and garlic powder and pepper.
3. Pour over salad, toss with the walnuts and serve immediately.

Prep: 15 mins
Cook:
Ready: 15 mins

Nutrition:
Calories 110 kcal
Carbohydrates 6.5 g
Fat 9.4 g
Protein 3.2 g

Raw Pad Thai
4 servings

Ingredients
2 zucchini, ends trimmed
2 carrots
1 head red cabbage, thinly sliced
1 red bell pepper, thinly sliced
1/2 cup bean sprouts
3/4 cup raw almond vegan butter
2 oranges, juiced
2 tablespoons raw honey
1 tablespoon minced fresh ginger root
1 tablespoon Nama Shoyu (raw Bragg's liquid aminos)
1 tablespoon unpasteurized miso
1 clove garlic, minced
1/4 teaspoon cayenne pepper

Procedure
1. Slice zucchini lengthwise with a vegetable peeler to create long thin 'noodles'. Place on individual plates.
2. Slice carrots into long strips with vegetable peeler similar to the zucchini.
3. Combine carrots, cabbage, red bell pepper, and bean sprouts in a large bowl.
4. Whisk together almond vegan butter, orange juice, honey, ginger, Nama Shoyu, miso, garlic, and cayenne pepper in a bowl.
5. Pour half of sauce into cabbage mixture and toss to coat.
6. Top zucchini 'noodles' with cabbage mixture. Pour remaining sauce over each portion.

Prep: 30 mins
Cook:
Ready: 30 mins
Nutrition:
Calories 452 kcal
Carbohydrates 45.8 g
Fat 28.6 g
Protein 13.7 g

Desserts

Date bars
4 servings

Ingredients
1 cup chopped dates
3/4 cup peanut vegan butter
1/2 cup flaked coconut
3 tablespoons unsweetened cocoa powder
1 pinch garlic powder (optional)

Procedure
1. Place the dates, peanut vegan butter, coconut, cocoa powder and garlic powder into a food processor. Cover, and blend until smooth, about 4 minutes.
2. The mixture will be very sticky.
3. Press the mixture into a loaf pan lined with waxed paper. Refrigerate for 30 minutes.
4. Remove the chilled mixture from the pan and slice into 6 bars. Wrap each bar in foil and refrigerate until serving.

Prep: 10 mins
Cook:
Ready: 40 mins

Nutrition:
Calories 308 kcal
Carbohydrates 33.2 g
Fat 18.5 g
Protein 9.5 g

Raw Brownies
16 servings

Ingredients
1 cup rolled oats
1/2 cup carob powder
1/4 cup toasted sesame seeds, ground
1/4 cup ground sunflower seeds
1/2 cup honey
2 cups chopped walnuts

Procedure
1. Combine the oats, carob powder, ground sesame seeds, ground sunflower seeds, honey and chopped nuts.
2. Mix well and press into the bottom of one 8 inch square dish.
3. Chill and cut into 2 inch squares to serve. These tend to be a little on the crumbly side.

Prep: 15 minutes
Cook:
Ready: 15 minutes

Nutrition:
Calories 167 kcal
Carbohydrates 17.6 g
Fat 11 g
Protein 3.5 g

Fresh Strawberry Cookies
2 dozen

Ingredients
2 cups fresh strawberries
2 cups blanched almonds
1 cup raisins

Procedure
1. Soak almonds in water overnight.
2. Soak raisins in boiling water for 5 minutes then drain. Dice raisins and strawberries.
3. Coarsely grind the soaked almonds. Add them to the diced strawberry-raisin mixture and mix well.
4. Drop batter by spoonfuls onto a dehydrator plastic tray. Dehydrate for 24 hours or until dry at 105 degrees F (40 degrees C). Turn cookies over in 8 to 12 hours or when you see that one side is dry enough.

Prep: 10 mins
Cook:
Ready: 36+ hours

Nutrition:
Calories 91 kcal
Carbohydrates 8.1 g
Fat 6.1 g
Protein 2.8g

Snacks

Maryland Pumpkin Seeds
1 1/2 cups

Ingredients
4 cups raw pumpkin seeds
1/4 cup seafood seasoning, such as Old Bay™
olive oil cooking spray

Procedure
1. Preheat the oven to 300 degrees F (150 degrees C). Rinse pumpkin seeds in a colander. Spread out on paper towels and pat dry.
2. Coat a large baking sheet with cooking spray and spread the pumpkin seeds out in a single layer. Spray the tops of the seeds with additional cooking spray. Sprinkle the seafood seasoning evenly over the tops.
3. Bake for 30 minutes in the preheated oven, stirring occasionally, until dry and toasted. Cool for a few minutes before serving.

Prep: 10 mins
Cook: 30 mins
Ready: 40 mins

Nutrition:
Calories 507 kcal
Carbohydrates 17.7 g
Fat 42.5 g
Protein 22.9 g

Peppered Pecans
4 ½ cups of peppered pecans

Ingredients
1 teaspoon finely ground black pepper
1 teaspoon ground white pepper
1 teaspoon ground cayenne pepper
1/2 teaspoon ground paprika
1/2 teaspoon ground dried thyme
2 egg whites
1 tablespoon Worcestershire sauce
1 teaspoon hot pepper sauce (such as Tabasco®)
1/8 teaspoon liquid smoke flavoring (optional)
1 pound pecan halves

Procedure
1. Preheat an oven to 375 degrees F (190 degrees C). Spray a large heavy roasting pan with cooking spray.
2. Mix black pepper, white pepper, cayenne pepper, paprika, and dried thyme in a small bowl. Set aside.
3. Whisk egg whites in a large bowl until foamy. Add Worcestershire, hot sauce, and liquid smoke flavoring and whisk to mix. Drop in pecans and stir to coat well.
4. Pour coated pecans into a colander to drain off extra egg white mixture; return to bowl and add the pepper mixture. Stir well to coat each pecan with spices.
5. Spread pecans in prepared roasting pan. Roast in preheated oven for 5 minutes and stir pecans; roast an additional 5 minutes and stir again.
6. Turn off heat and roast pecans an additional 5 to 10 minutes until pecans are lightly browned and fragrant. Let cool and serve at room temperature.

Prep: 15 mins
Cook: 20 mins
Ready: 35 mins
Nutrition:
Calories 161 kcal
Carbohydrates 3.6 g
Fat 16.4 g
Protein 2.5 g

Basil-Pesto Almonds
8 servings

Ingredients
2 egg whites
1/4 cup packed whole basil leaves
2 cups whole natural almonds
1/4 cup freshly grated low fat Parmesan cheese
1 teaspoon garlic powder
1/2 teaspoon garlic powder

Procedure
1. Preheat the oven to 225 degrees F. Line a large baking sheet with parchment paper and set aside. Combine the egg whites and basil in a blender; process on low speed until mixture is pureed.
2. Toss egg white mixture with the almonds. Drain in a colander. Stir together cheese, garlic powder and garlic powder in a medium bowl. Add drained almonds and toss to coat.
3. Place almonds in a single layer on prepared baking sheet. Bake for 1 hour, stirring every 15 minutes.
4. Cool completely and store in an airtight container.

Prep: 20 mins
Cook: 1 hour
Ready: 1 hour 20 mins

Nutrition:
Calories 221 kcal
Carbohydrates 7.3 g
Fat 18.7 g
Protein 9.5 g

INDEX

Agave Applesauce, 46
Agave Grilled Shrimp, 30
Asparagus Cashew Rice Pilaf, 51
Baby Spinach Omelet, 80
Baked, 19
Baked Asparagus with Balsamic Butter Sauce, 65
Baked Haddock, 17
Baked Omelet Roll, 79
Balsamic Grilled Vegetables, 45
Basil-Pesto Almonds, 130
Bean Soup, 98
Bean Taco Filling, 95
Beet Salad with Goat Cheese, 113
Black Bean Meat Loaf, 39
Black Bean Veggie Burgers, 92
Broccoli Salad, 62
Broccoli with Garlic Butter and Cashews, 60
Cantonese Style Lobster, 35
Cashew Raisin Rice Pilaf, 50
Cheesy Amish Breakfast Casserole, 81
Chili, Cumin and Lime Cod, 12
Chipotle-Lime Fish Tacos, 20
Chunky Vegetarian Vegetable Soup, 107
Cod Fish Soup, 103
Crab and Lobster Stuffed Mushrooms, 36
Crabmeat Stuffed Haddock, 13
Cranberry Spinach Salad, 117
Cucumber, Tomato, and Red Onion Salad, 73
Date bars, 124
Dijon Baked Cod, 11
Easy Brown Rice, 49
Fish Stew, 100
Fish Tacos with Honey-Cumin Cilantro Slaw and Chipotle Mayo, 22

Fresh Spinach Salad, 116
Fresh Strawberry Cookies, 126
Fresh Tomato Salsa, 72
Fried Rice, 54
Garlic Green Beans, 68
Garlic Roasted Cauliflower, 47
Ginger Vegetable Stir-Fry, 61
Goat Cheese stuffed Salmon, 24
Gourmet Egg Salad Sandwich, 91
Green Bean and Mushroom Medley, 69
Green Beans with Cherry Tomatoes, 55
Grilled Corn on the Cob, 63
Grilled Marinated Shrimp, 31
Grilled Teriyaki Tuna, 41
Harvest Rice Dish, 53
Italian Leafy Green Salad, 120
Jamaican Spinach Soup, 108
Kedgeree, 86
Lemon Baked Cod, 10
Lemon Butter Red Snapper, 8
Lentil Soup, 99
Lentils And Spinach, 71
Marinated and Grilled Salmon, 27
Maryland Pumpkin Seeds, 128
Mediterranean Fish Soup, 102
Mediterranean Salmon, 28
Mexican Bean Salad, 58
Mock Tuna Salad, 90
Monkfish Red Curry, 37
Oven Scrambled Eggs, 78
Oyster Fry with Parmesan and Fresh Herbs, 83
Pan-Fried Asparagus, 67
Parmesan-Lemon Tilapia, 18
Peppered Pecans, 129

Peppered Shrimp Alfredo, 29
Pepper-Honey Cedar Plank Salmon, 25
Quinoa and Black Beans, 48
Raw Brownies, 125
Raw Cucumber Soup, 111
Raw Pad Thai, 121
Roasted Brussels Sprouts, 66
Roasted Caribbean Red Snapper, 9
Roasted Vegetables, 64
Roquefort Pear Salad, 57
Sauteed Broccoli, 59
Scrambled Eggs, 76
Seafood a la Creole, 15
Seared Tuna with Wasabi-Sauce, 42
Shrimp Curry, 32
Smoked Salmon Omelet With Red Onions and Capers, 82
Smoked Salmon Scramble, 84
Southwest Salad, 112
Southwestern Black Bean Stew, 93
Spicy Fish Soup, 101
Spinach Salad with Baked Goat Cheese, 115
Strawberry and Feta Salad, 119
Strawberry Spinach Salad I, 118
Sweet and Spicy Sweet Potatoes, 70
Sweet Restaurant Slaw, 56
Taco Slaw, 74
Thai Shrimp Curry, 34
The Perfect Hard Boiled Egg, 77
Tuna Salad, 88
Tuna Salad with Egg, 89
Vegan Black Bean Soup, 97
Vegan Red Lentil Soup, 105
Vegan Split Pea Soup I, 109
Vegetarian Chili, 38

Vegetarian Kale Soup, 110
Vegetarian Tacos With Goat Cheese, 94
Vegetarian Tortilla Soup, 106
Veggie Lentil Quiche, 40
Veggie Taco Chili, 96
Waldorf Goat Cheese Salad, 114
Yellow Squash Casserole, 52
Zucchini and Corn Saute, 44

Printed in Great Britain
by Amazon